9 R.U.L.E.S TO GEOSPATIAL CONSULTING

How to Recognize Your Potential, Create Value, and Become a Trusted Geospatial Consultant

Dinesh Kar

INDIA • SINGAPORE • MALAYSIA

Notion Press

No.8, 3rd Cross Street,
CIT Colony, Mylapore,
Chennai, Tamil Nadu – 600004

First Published by Notion Press 2021
Copyright © Dinesh Kar 2021
All Rights Reserved.

ISBN 978-1-63806-616-3

This book has been published with all efforts taken to make the material error-free after the consent of the author. However, the author and the publisher do not assume and hereby disclaim any liability to any party for any loss, damage, or disruption caused by errors or omissions, whether such errors or omissions result from negligence, accident, or any other cause.

While every effort has been made to avoid any mistake or omission, this publication is being sold on the condition and understanding that neither the author nor the publishers or printers would be liable in any manner to any person by reason of any mistake or omission in this publication or for any action taken or omitted to be taken or advice rendered or accepted on the basis of this work. For any defect in printing or binding the publishers will be liable only to replace the defective copy by another copy of this work then available.

Disclaimer

The information provided within this book is for general informational and educational purposes only. The author makes no representations or warranties, express or implied, about the completeness, accuracy, reliability, suitability, or availability concerning the information, products, services, or related graphics contained in this book for any purpose. Any use of this information is at your own risk.

Any names or characters, businesses or places, events, or incidents, are fictitious. Any resemblance to actual persons, living or dead, or actual events is purely coincidental.

This memoir is a truthful recollection of actual events in the author's life. Some conversations have been recreated and/or supplemented. The names and details of some individuals have been changed to respect their privacy.

Dedication

I warmly dedicate this book to my mother Mukti Lata Kar and my father, Late Dr. Debendra Nath Kar

And

I passionately dedicate this to you all readers

Contents

Preface 9

Acknowledgment 15

Section 1: Recognize

Chapter 1	Recognizing Self Potential	19
Chapter 2	Transformation of Skillset to Consulting Mindset	41
Chapter 3	Nine Myths of Consulting	53

Section 2: Uncover

Chapter 4	Nine Specific Skills of Geospatial Consultant	65

Section 3: Learn

Chapter 5	Consulting Framework	97
Chapter 6	Approach to Consultative Selling	113

Section 4: Engage

Chapter 7	Nine Motives to Become Geospatial Consultant	135
Chapter 8	Nine Forms of Consultancy and Consulting Business	147

Section 5: Secure

Chapter 9   Risks and Rewards of Consulting................................ 157

Chapter 10   Reason of Consulting Business Failure..................... 169

Move to Problem Solving Action – Start Consulting 183

References.. 185

Preface

Dear readers, it is my heartfelt gratitude to you for being part of this transforming journey. I have been preaching on the importance of the application of geospatial technology in agriculture to students, researchers, and professionals. The technology should not only be considered as a tool of map-making and data creation whereas it must be used for information analysis, planning, and effective decision making.

My first book "*Sensing Agriculture from Space*" detailed about what are the solutions for key players in the agriculture value chain. This book is on the person "who" can provide geospatial solutions. In the geospatial industry, three types of experts are observed working in agriculture projects. The first type which is in majority is the GIS experts who have gained some knowledge of image processing & analysis by working in agriculture-based projects. These experts from different backgrounds such as engineering, geography, science graduates with geoinformatics, etc. The second type is agriculture experts who are working in agriculture-based projects having limited or no skills in GIS. They take the support of GIS experts to create any output. These experts are mostly hired externally by companies to provide domain knowledge support to the project. The third types are very few in the industry and these are Agriculture experts having bachelor, or master's, or even doctorate degrees in agriculture sciences and have working experience in GIS & Remote Sensing. This category of experts is particularly important as they can bridge the gap between the client's needs and providing a solution to the needs. However, all these three categories of experts are spending most of their time and effort in data creation for clients.

The purpose of this book is to create a consulting mindset for these categories of experts, transform them from the mindset of a skilled expert to problem-solving consultants and make them the *"trusted expert" or "leading light"*. The book is written with examples around individuals from the industry of Agriculture, and GIS because that is the world I know.

Having expertise in a GIS and Agriculture contributes to reputation, credibility, and acceptance to one's branding in the Geospatial as well as the Agribusiness sector. To be a consultant in geospatial agribusiness translates into being successful and can provide value to the company as well as to clients.

A geospatial agriculture consultant can play an important role in the use of technology for solving problems of key stakeholders in the agriculture value chain. Geospatial agriculture consultant bridges the gap between the agriculture company and technology service providers. He/She can have a dual role such as "Agriculture Consultant in Geospatial Company" and as "Geospatial Consultant in Agriculture Company".

> *"The purpose of human life is to serve, and to show compassion and the will to help others."*
>
> **– Albert Schweitzer**

This book delivers the keys to the success of specialized consulting in the geospatial agribusiness sector. This book is written for professionals and experts with Agriculture and Geospatial (GIS/RS/GPS) knowledge, experience, and expertise, who wish to shift from an employee skillset to a consulting mindset. The shift in the consulting mindset can create a different approach to working. This book can be useful for:

- *GIS & remote sensing professionals who are debating leaving corporate life and want to explore an alternative lifestyle.*

- *GIS & remote sensing professionals who are working part-time and want to get recognized as a consulting expert.*

- *Agriculture professionals with GIS skillset who want to establish their own consulting business and increase their market share.*

- *Agriculture GIS experts who want to begin an independent lifestyle.*

- *GIS experts who are spending their time and effort in data creation and wants to shift to problem-solving as an internal or external consultant to increase revenue for the company and value for the client.*

This book can be helpful to individuals who are stuck in employment and are not able to use their skills to the full potential. This group of highly technical individuals would always be dreaming to live a life portrayed below:

- *Having flexibility and true freedom.*

- *Work to reach your full potential.*

- *Become your boss.*

- *Choose how much you want to earn.*

- *Having the liberty to choose your client and projects you like.*

This book is a step-by-step guide to transform an individual to get into a consulting mindset. I have used two key elements in this book, the first one is RULES, and the Second element is number "9".

The book is divided into five sections and is been given acronym as "RULES", which means:

R – Recognize your potential for consulting.

U – Uncover the skills and qualities required to be a trusted expert.

L – Learn the framework and approach to become an expert/consultant.

E – Engage by learning the reasons and modes of consulting.

S – Secure from risks and reasons for failures in consulting.

The number "NINE" depicts the points in each chapter.

The first stage of consulting is recognition of self-potential and transforming a professional from a working skillset to a consulting mindset. This section deals with the definition of consulting and bringing clarity on nine myths of consulting.

The second stage of consulting is to uncover consulting skills and qualities that a professional must have to create value for the customer and become indispensable in geospatial agribusiness. This is one of the key sections of the book. In this, there are sub-sections on nine essential qualities of a trusted consultant, nine steps of consulting framework, nine steps to become a consultant or to start a consulting business, and nine techniques of consultative selling.

The third stage is learning. Once the self-potential is identified and the qualities of a consultant are practiced, then a professional must learn the consultative selling approach and consulting framework. The framework teaches how to build a relation till closing the project.

The fourth stage of consulting is modes of getting engaged as a consultant. Nine different modes of consulting, their advantages and disadvantages are explained in this section. This section also describes the nine reasons that drive an individual to go for a consulting approach to working.

The fifth stage of the book details the security measures that consultants must be aware of. In this section, the chapters are on nine reasons to be kept in mind, why consultants fail and nine risks and rewards to be a consultant. In this, the chapters are on nine types of people who can become a consultant and nine reasons for them to become a consultant. Followed by this, there is a chapter on nine types of consulting business.

In this book, I do not want to teach Agriculture subjects or techniques of GIS & remote sensing. I have emphasized the qualities and understanding required to become a *"Geospatial Agriculture Consultant"*. These qualities are learned through the experience of working in the geospatial industry.

The consulting steps, approaches, and qualities are presented as a story. The lead character of the story is Mr. Dev who is a *"Geospatial Agriculture Consultant"* and is sharing his experience in this book. He spent two decades of his career working as remote sensing and GIS expert for agriculture projects. Throughout his career, he has worked in Agriculture projects only and used RS & GIS techniques to fulfill the scope of work of the projects. During this period, he executed about fifty projects, visited eight different countries as an expert. After getting the complete exposure, experience, expertise, he decided to get into consulting. For the past six years, he is not only involved in executing projects, but he is also adding value to projects, solving the problems of clients, defining the solutions to the problems, and implementing the solution with the client. He has trained about two-hundred students, researchers, and professionals in GIS applications for agriculture. He realized the value of problem-solving, the joy of serving, the satisfaction of taking your client from the current (low) stage to a higher stage, and enjoying your time with family and friends.

This book is presented as a story of Mr. Dev's journey from being an efficient and hardworking skillset transforming into the mindset of agriculture consultant with a purpose to solve agriculture problems for the agribusiness sector using geospatial technology.

> *"Nothing sticks in your head better than a story. Stories can express the most complicated ideas in the most digestible ways."*
>
> **– Sam Balter**

After reading this book you will have the clarity on:

- Why should you get into geospatial agriculture consulting?
- How can you transform yourself into a consultant in Geospatial agriculture?
- When should you start consulting for geospatial agriculture?
- What are the qualities and skills required to become a trusted geospatial agriculture consultant?

As an author, my mission is to develop many more geospatial agriculture consultants through training and coaching. I thank once again all the readers to join me on my purpose to transform from the mode of *"**Work and Earn**"* to *"**Serve and Grow**"*.

> *"Every year in consulting is like three years in the corporate world because you have multiple clients, multiple issues - you grow so much"*
>
> **– Indra Nooyi**

Acknowledgment

First and foremost, praises and thanks to the god, the almighty, for his showers of blessings throughout my journey of learning in the profession. In the process of putting this book together, I realized how true this gift of writing is for me. You give me the power to believe in my passion and pursue my dreams. I could never have done this without the faith I have in you, the Almighty.

Writing a book is harder than I thought and more gratifying than I could have ever anticipated. None of this would have been possible without my wife, my son, and my mother. They stood by me during every struggle and all my successes. I am eternally grateful to my brothers, who always encouraged me to learn and supported my hunger to grow.

My time in the industry would not have been made possible without the esteemed organizations I worked for, projects I was part of, and the places I visited. To all the individuals I have had the opportunity to lead, be led by, or watch their leadership from afar, I want to say thank you for being the inspiration.

Without the experiences and support from my friends, this book would not exist. You have allowed me to continue my consulting, teaching, training, and especially the learning process.

My additional thanks to everyone in the publishing team who completed this book and helping more authors turn their thoughts into stories.

Section 1

Recognize

Recognize Uncover Learn Engage Secure

Chapter 1

Recognizing Self Potential

"Once your mindset changes, everything on the outside will change along with it"

– Steve Maraboli

The future of professional services is all about expertise, people, and relationship. One must gain the most amount of knowledge to promote oneself as an expert. People and organizations will look at the expert as a trusted resource to provide the solutions they need. Consulting services is all about relationship. In one of Dan Lok's presentations, he says, "Client does not take your service because of what you sell, but because of who you are. There is no transactional relationship in consulting but there is always a transformational relationship between client and expert". Knowledge alone is not sufficient to become a "trusted consultant" or "the leading light". Knowledge with the ability to use with good judgment is of importance.

Most of the professionals will have questions like-

"I have the subject knowledge and experience. How can I be considered a consultant?"

"I have knowledge and experience of handling client projects but why am I not given value as an expert in the team?"

"How do I become a consultant with no experience?"

"I do not have long years of experience and high education. Can I still be considered as a consultant within a company?"

These are typical questions that arise and if they are not answered, individuals continue to work as a cog in the company and become replaceable. The most important question they will have is "How can I add value to the project or company or the customer and thereby become an indispensable professional?".

Most of us do not start our careers as consultants, but we become a consultant over a period with skills and experiences. This does not mean that all who have skills and experience become a consultant. Only those who aspire to become one and develop the qualities to meet the consulting requirements get into consulting.

Let us understand this from the perspective of a geospatial organization. We start our career as a fresher having either domain knowledge or remote sensing & GIS knowledge. This is the first stage of our career, where most of our activities are restricted to the tasks assigned by managers. (*please refer to the diagram given below*). In this stage, we learn or develop additional skillset, such as domain expert learns tools and techniques of remote sensing. Similarly, RS or GIS experts learn the concepts of a domain in which he is working. He moves to the next stage by developing these additional skills. This is stage 2 which is senior analyst level, where the tasks are mostly restricted to the scope of the project assigned. If anyone does not add skills to his portfolio at stage 1, then he continues to grow in "path 1" with some minimal benefits. These people are highly vulnerable as they can be easily replaced by other freshers having the same or better skills.

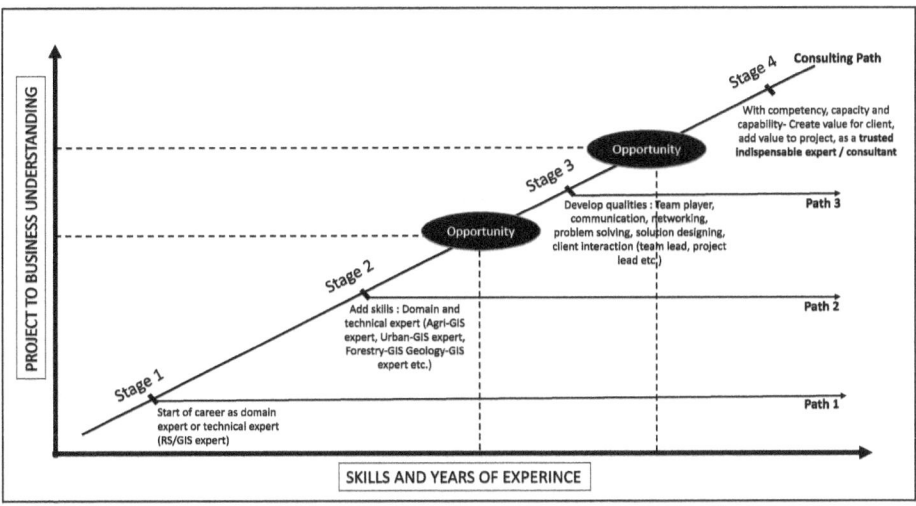

Further from senior analysts, if one develops the qualities of problem identification and solving, team player, communication and listening, networking, client handling, and integrity then he moves to stage three. Till stage one and two, the work is towards the project or work assigned to an individual. Whereas in stage three, the responsibility increases from guiding team, managing team, interacting with the client, and deliverable to the client. At this stage also if anyone, who focuses only on self-skills and team management then he gets into path three. This path is of managers, where project and team management are required. These people do not face the client at any stage of the project.

Stage four is the consulting or advisory role, wherewith all the technical skills, work qualities, and experiences, he works on understanding the client problem, defining the solution, implementing the solution, managing the team, working with partners, and delivering the results to the client. This all happens through relationship building with the client and team members. At this stage client trusts, this individual narrates their problem to get the best solution from the consultant.

During our career path, we get opportunities where we need to recognize the potential, we must become a consultant. (refer to the same figure above). These opportunities come at different stages and in various forms. For example

- CEO meeting senior analyst and asks, "One of my known clients, is facing this technical challenge, will you be able to provide any solution to this?"
- Sales and bidding team requesting management for the support of a technical expert to work on the client's proposal.
- Sales team asking a technical expert to visit and understand the client's requirements.
- Bidding team asking for the support of an expert to attend the pre-bid meeting and understand the request for proposal.
- Head of the departments and managers asking a qualified technical person to visit a client for delivering the results and present the project.

These are some examples of the opportunities that we get during our careers. In all such cases, an aspiring consultant will take the opportunity and work on it. If he is not skilled enough, he diverts the request to another competent person.

Becoming a Geospatial consultant requires integration of technical expertise (domain and GIS knowledge), experience (working in small or big projects), and interpersonal skills.

An instance that may illustrate this point.

A little more than nine years ago, it was a hot summer month in India, Dev was traveling to Addis Ababa, Ethiopia which is one of the East African countries. Dev was a Project Lead (GIS) at that time and was leading a team of twelve members. Dev was asked by the sales team and management to present the technical part of the proposal that is submitted. It was his second international trip but the first solo international trip. The sales team decided to support over email and phone in case of any requirements. He was nervous and excited to visit a new country. A couple of months before this travel, Dev's company had submitted a proposal to a client in Addis Ababa who was leading the proposal for the Ministry of Agriculture. Dev's company and another company from Europe were the associated partners. Dev's company role was as a GIS technical mapping partner, the European company's role was Quality checking of Maps and reports received from Dev's Company and the local Ethiopian company's role was field survey, data collection, client coordination, and submission of reports. This was a proposal discussion meeting with the team and then with a technical team from the Ministry of Agriculture (MoA) to shortlist the company for project execution, to finalize the roles, project timelines, deliverables. Dev's company chose a low-cost route as the amount was not part of any project and must be taken from the business unit sales budget.

This travel was no less than any adventure trip for Dev. The trip had multiple flight changes, which was making him more excited. Dev is from the City of Hyderabad, located in the state of Telangana, India. His company booked his itinerary. Dev had to take first a domestic flight to Mumbai which was by Indian Airlines. From Mumbai, the next destination was Dubai by Emirates Airlines, followed by this was Nairobi (Kenya) by Kenya Airways, and then finally to Addis Ababa (Ethiopia) by again Kenya Airways. Dev started his journey by taking the afternoon flight to Mumbai. The next flight to Dubai was at midnight so he decided to spend his time at the airport. He spent his time watching people going and coming. Some struggling with their large size suitcases pushing the cart, some sleeping on the floor, some sleeping above the luggage itself, few were busy reading books, and few were found moving around airport duty shops. Once the immigration check was over and Dev was waiting for boarding, he started talking to people sitting next to him waiting.

He found that most of them were going to middle east countries like Saudi Arabia, Kuwait, Bahrain, and Muscat. Some for business and some returning to their work after holidays. After he boarded the flight had the snacks and drinks provided on board and then went asleep. When he woke up, he found that night was over, and the sun was slowly rising and making the flight cabin brighter. He had coffee, that was offered onboard and started thinking about his next destination. Dev was still in his excitement mode as he was to spend eight hours in Dubai Airport in Transit. He has heard a lot about Dubai airport and has done some research on the internet. After reaching Dubai airport, Dev spent his time in the shopping area, getting into every shop, looking at the item, their prices, and converting in Indian rupees. The airport terminal with the shopping area is around one and a half kilometers in length. Dev might have done about three to four rounds going from one end to the other. Dev was making note of things he wanted to buy so that on his return trip he will buy all those. Dev was incredibly happy to find as if the entire world was there at the airport. He could see people from all over the world, and from different countries. Their looks were different, their dresses were different, their skin colors were different, and their languages were different.

After spending more than five hours roaming in the airport, Dev got tired and decided to take a rest. He spotted a relaxing seat and lied there to take a short nap. Within a few minutes, he woke up and switched on his laptop. Now his mind got into work mode. He opened the presentation he prepared for the meeting at Addis Ababa. He went through the slides about a couple of times, made some notes, and kept back the laptop in the bag. He went to have coffee. While moving towards the Coffee shop he went through the display boards where the flight timings and gate numbers are displayed. He was shocked to find that his flight to Nairobi was delayed by two hours. He was worried now as he may miss the connecting flight from Nairobi to Addis Ababa. He went to the inquiry counter to make the confirmation. He had two hours of transit time in Nairobi as per the itinerary, but now he was worried as with the delay of two hours he is going to miss the flight. The itinerary was shared with the client where the client had arranged for pickup at the airport. Other passengers were also found enquiring about the same. Dev went to them and asked about the next action. Dev introduced himself to one of them and told his concern. He also introduced himself. His name was Solomon. He worked for an international NGO in the education sector. He was a regular traveler and said, "My friend, this happens most of the time. At Nairobi they will arrange something. If there is any next flight with vacant seats, then they will put you in that. Do not worry brother".

Dev was relaxed and amazed by the words of Solomon. Within just a few minutes of interaction, a person from a different continent and different country tells you, friend and brother. He learned that, if you want to earn respect, you must give respect. And the second thing he noticed was that if you are modest with others, you can make a lot of friends from any part of the world.

Dev went to the Coffee shop and had the Ethiopian Bean coffee. It was the first time he was tasting African bean coffee. The aroma was so nice. He was able to smell when the chef was making the coffee. The chef told him that, people from Africa take this coffee without milk and with brown sugar. Dev also decided to have in the same way. He took the first sip and was so lip-smacking that he cannot express. He took the coffee and went back to a relaxing seat preparing his words and sentences for the presentation.

Dev had spent twelve years in the GIS industry. He was then designated in his company as a GIS Team Lead. He was managing a team of fifteen members. His team had remote sensing analysts, GIS engineers, and business development executives. Dev's role was to execute projects and support the sales team in preparing technical documents for any proposal. For this specific client visit, he was briefed by his seniors on the topic he should present to the client and not get into any financial commitments. The work was on preparing region-wise thematic maps of land use land cover, drainage and stream network, slope, and Soil at 1:50,000 scale for the country. He started preparing his talk on methodologies for all the thematic mapping objectives, the classes for each theme, support that will be required from the local team, and deliverable mechanism.

After a couple of hours spending again moving in airport duty-free shops, the boarding stated. Inside the aircraft, Dev went through the aisle and found Solomon in flight. He wished him and Solomon again reassured Dev and said, "not to worry friend, everything will be alright. Have a nice journey and stay".

The real surprise and adventure were when the flight landed at Nairobi airport. When Dev and other passengers were deplaning, he found some ground staff standing with placards as Addis Ababa, Maputo, Dar-es-Salaam, Kampala. They were also shouting by these place names. After hearing Addis Ababa, Dev raised his hand and was asked to wait next to the ground staff holding placard of Addis Ababa. Dev asked him, about the matter. The ground staff said, your next flight to Addis Ababa is ready to take off. Some passengers from this flight will be taken there directly and then it will take off. For Dev, it was all sounding like a movie. After a few minutes, about eight passengers were taken in a van. This van was passing through several aircraft. The ground staff looked at passenger's passports, boarding passes and checked in the papers she was holding. Within a few minutes, these passengers were near the aircraft which was to go to Addis Ababa. It was the same flight that Dev was booked in and was worried about missing. Dev took a deep breath, smiled at the staff, and thanked her for the help. He enjoyed every moment after that. He started talking to a fellow passenger on the flight. It was a two-hour short flight. Dev finally reached his destination. The vehicle was waiting at the exit gate with the chauffeur holding placard by Dev's name. He was taken to the hotel. The hotel appeared to be a luxurious star hotel. Dev first called the client and informed him about his safe arrival. The client asked him to take a rest for the day and to meet the next day. He also assured Dev that, a vehicle will be sent to pick him in the morning. Dev checked in to the room, took bath, and came down to the lobby, where he sat to observe people and understand them. He went through some of the magazines that were kept for the guests. He then moved around the hotel passing the restaurant, swimming pool area, gym area, discussion cabins, conference halls, and so on. After about an hour, he went back to his room on the fourteenth floor and started working on the presentation again. He took an early dinner and went to sleep by 8 PM. This might be due to the time difference of two and a half hours between India and Ethiopia.

The next morning

Dev woke up early as he slept early and might be due to the time difference. He was on the breakfast table by 7 AM. After finishing the breakfast, Dev went back to his room got ready for the meeting that was scheduled at 9 AM.

At 8:20 AM Dev gets a call in the room. From the other side, there is a gentle voice of a lady and she said, "Mr. Dev, this is Ayana from Daniel's office. The vehicle has come to pick you. Please come by 8:30 AM"

Dev responded immediately and said, "I am ready Ayana and I will be there at the lobby in two minutes". Dev reaches the lobby and finds a beautiful girl, who appeared to be in her late twenties or earlier thirties, dressed in blue jeans, high heels leather shoes, a slim-fit t-shirt, and a headscarf tied in the neck. She was looking no less than any model. She introduces herself to Dev and greets him with a handshake and a nice half shoulder hug.

"Good Morning Ayana", Said Dev and continued. "Shall we proceed, or do we need to wait for some more time?"

"Well, we will wait for some more time. My colleague has gone to the restaurant to get Mr. Jason who has also arrived last night from the Netherlands", responded Ayana.

"That is nice. Can we sit and talk? I would be thankful to you if you can tell me about yourself, your colleagues and about your office" Dev asked Ayana.

"Sure Mr. Dev," said Ayana

"Well, I am a forestry expert and looking after forestry-related projects in Daniel's office. I am working with Daniel for the past four years. I joined Daniel after I completed graduation in Forestry. In addition to that, I support the preparation of bids and proposals for the company. This bid, in which we are going to work for the Ministry of Agriculture is also prepared by me". Ayana answered. "My colleague Samuel is a GIS Expert and has done a geoinformatics course from ITC Netherlands. He recently completed his course and joined Daniel's office about four months back. He knows Mr. Jason and that is why he has gone personally to get him here."

She smiled and said, "I know about you also, Mr. Dev, as I have prepared the proposal document where all the expert CVs were incorporated". Ayana said. "You are an Agriculture expert having expertise in Geospatial Technology with more than ten years of experience".

"You can call me Dev. How about Mr. Jason". Dev enquired.

"Mr. Jason is also a forestry expert with more than twenty-five years of experience. He has worked on many projects in multiple countries. All his projects are using remote sensing and Geographic Information Systems (GIS). He is going to be a Quality assurance and Quality Checking consultant for all the map outputs that will be created by your organization Mr. Dev."

"Please address me as Dev else I will also call you Miss Ayana".

"Ok, Sorry Dev", responded Ayana.

"This is so nice to know about the team, Ayana. It will be very delightful to work with you all". Said Dev.

"Yes, we all hope so. The contract is yet to be finalized. Although Daniel has good connections in Ministry, as he has done a couple of projects with them. Daniel is also a close friend of a Director in Ministry. There is still some gap in understanding with project requirements and our deliverables on which the ministry team would like to discuss with our executing team. Hence this meeting is called" stated Ayana.

Dev said to Ayana, "It is already 8:40 AM, shall we walk and wait near the vehicle. Else we may spend some more time introducing with Mr. Jason and Mr. Samuel. We can have our introduction in the vehicle."

"Yes, that will be nice. Let us walk. I Hope, it is fine with you. Otherwise, once Samuel is here, he can get the vehicle to the hotel lobby area", asked Ayana.

"That is perfectly fine with me", said Dev.

While both Dev and Ayana were walking and about to reach the vehicle, that was parked fifty to sixty meters away, they heard a voice from the back. It was Samuel calling Ayana to stop.

Dev immediately went to Samuel and gave a handshake and introduced himself. Samuel apologized for the delay and the walk. Dev said to him that "we are field people and weather is also pleasant here. I only advised Ayana for the walk".

Samuel was a young energetic boy wearing jeans and black blazers. The light blue shirt inside the blazers was giving a good formal look. Samuel opened the car door with his remote key and requested Ayana and Dev to sit in the backseat so that Mr. Jason can be in the front seat. He said, "I will take the one-way U-turn and pick Mr. Jason from the hotel lobby area. He is waiting there".

Samuel got into the driving wheel. It was red color Isuzu, a five-seater with a carrier at back. He drove to the hotel lobby area. Dev could see Mr. Jason from a distance. He was fair and tall. A well-built personality. He was holding a small laptop bag, a spiral notebook, and a water bottle. He was wearing cream color trousers and half sleeves white shirt that was making him look ever fairer.

Mr. Jason got in the car and greeted all with Good Morning and shook hands with Dev and Ayana. Dev and Mr. Jason exchanged words about their travel and decided to meet in the evening as they are in the same hotel.

The first part of a series of technical meetings

At 09:15 AM, Daniel enters the conference room, where Dev, Mr. Jason, Ayana, and Samuel were present. He greets Dev, Samuel, and Mr. Jason with a firm handshake. And greets Ayana with a handshake clubbed with a hug. Daniel calls for some black coffee and cookies for the team. He starts with the agenda of the day, where they will have an internal meeting in the first half, followed by lunch, and then will move to the Agriculture Director's office in the building of the Ministry of Agriculture.

For a couple of hours, they had presentations that were like a practice session. Daniel detailed about who will speak when and who will answer if any question is raised by the director etc. Dev's presentation was longer as it had many methodologies with some data required from the Department of Agriculture. Hence, they decided Dev and Ayana to present together. Dev to present complete slides and whenever any support is asked, then Ayana will step in and put a request to Director and understand the procedure to get those data.

The preparatory round went well and at 12:30 Noon, they all went for lunch. In lunch, Dev could find that almost all were grabbing bread, chicken, and a lot of ice-filled cold drinks. Dev took a small bowl of rice, with pulse gravy, fried potato, chips, and water. Followed by the lunch, then again had Coffee.

Post lunch, meeting at Director's office of the Ministry of Agriculture

The meeting started at 2:00 PM. As was prepared, the meeting went smoothly. Dev's presentation went for more than an hour as Director and his technical team understood the approach and agreed to all the support that will be required for the project. The paper-work procedures were explained to Ayana. Dev has a quality of attracting the audience with his smile and making the presentation interactive with questions and answers.

After the meeting was over, Director invited the team for snacks arranged at his office. At his office, he offered tea with milk to Dev and coffee for rest. Dev was surprised by this. On this Director said, "I know Indians like tea more than Coffee and especially in Hyderabad, you have special Irani Chai. I once visited Hyderabad for a conference and liked the hospitality of Indian people". Dev was happy to know this and enjoyed the tea with milk and sugar.

Daniel took permission from the Director for leaving and again meeting them the next day with Agriculture Minister. To Daniel's surprise, the Director request some time from Dev so that he can take him to the data lab and show a similar type of work done ten years earlier. Daniel was pleased as Director is personally showing the data that would have been difficult for the team to get. Director took Dev and the team to the lab. Now Dev was slowly opening-up after looking at the data. He requested the Director If he can ask some questions related to the current project. On getting permission, Dev asked two questions.

"What was the objective five years ago to carry out the data creation work?" and

"What is the purpose of the current year's project? How is the department going to use the data that will be generated using the latest satellite images?"

To Dev's questions, the Director replied.

Ten years ago, the work was assigned to a company from Southeast Asia. It took two years then to generate countrywide thematic maps on land use land cover, soil, drainage patterns river and stream network, contours, and geomorphology. Using these maps mainly land use land cover, we have allotted lands to investors for agriculture development.

The purpose of the current year is like what it was five years ago. The change is on the size of land to be allotted. Because it was observed that, the companies who have invested in the land have not taken any action on the complete land. Some have done but they did not get the production as was expected. Some have changed the crop from what was presented to us. This might be due to financial and human resource problems to manage large pieces of land. Hence, we decided to go for updating and generating new maps so that new land can be allotted to new and existing investors.

Dev again asked, "What are the criteria for allotting the land to investors?"

Non-cultivated land, Non-forested land, lands with fewer habitations are some of the main criteria to allot the land. Director answered. We aim to utilize the land, generate employment for locals, and improve the livelihood of people.

Dev request to make some suggestion on this. Director permitted.

Dev said, "I am a geospatial Agriculture Expert, and hence I will speak as an agriculture expert for the geospatial team and as a geospatial expert for the agriculture team. Director Sir, I feel we should take this project to next level. Rather than only generating the data, we should also analyze the data. As I understand, the earlier investors may not have a problem with finances or other resources, but the reason could have been different. If we can use all these data that will be generated and carry-out land evaluation, then it will give us an idea of that land that is suitable for agriculture and land that is not suitable for agriculture. Again, in suitable land, we can have its category as highly suitable, moderately suitable, and slightly suitable.

Sounds good Dev, Director responded.

Dev said this is not enough Sir. Once we know the land is suitable, then we should carry out crop suitability for all the major crops and fruits that are grown in the country. This will give an idea of which crops can be grown on which piece of land. Hence if the crop and area match the investor's requirement, then it can be allotted to them. This will not make them struggle to grow a crop that is not suitable for that piece of land. For this, we have the requirement of climatic data, soil quality information, and other supporting information.

Director reacted "That is absolutely what we are looking at Dev. And this is where we were held-up to get more recommendations from the vendors. Daniel, I feel you have the right team to work on this. But we still must follow the bid procedure. I will put up the points that Dev has mentioned with the Minister. If he allows, we can discuss this at our next meeting".

Daniel then took leave from the Director's office and brought the team back to their Hotel. He categorically told Dev not to go out of the hotel in the night. And if he feels like having Indian food, then he can call Daniel so that he will take him to the Indian Hotel. To this Dev said, "Thank you for this. We will have some other day. Tonight, I and Mr. Jason will be discussing the project and have planned to have dinner together".

To this Daniel said, "I will join you both at 7:30 PM tonight for the dinner".

After dropping them, Daniel took permission from Mr. Jason and Dev, so that he can drop Samuel and Ayana also to their respective residence. This is an incredibly good quality of Daniel that Dev observed. He takes care of the team very well. Dev said bye to all. To this Ayana responded with a lovely smile, "Take care Dev and have a good sleep. See you tomorrow".

It was 5:30 PM when Dev reached his room. He took a shower. He spoke with his family in India about the day. He told them about the people he met places he visited, and the food he ate, etc.

In the restaurant at Dinner time

It was 7:30 PM, Dev went to the poolside restaurant of the hotel. After five minutes, Daniel joined him. Daniel made a call to Mr. Jason and asked him to come to the poolside restaurant. Daniel appeared to be relaxed after the meeting and his full day of work.

"I am sorry Dev; I could not ask about your travel and stay since morning. How is your stay here? If there is any problem do let me know, then we can shift to another hotel". Daniel said to Dev

"This is a perfect place and the hotel is fine. I am enjoying it here. You do not worry Daniel." Dev responded to Daniel.

After about five to seven minutes of their discussion Jason arrived. Jason looked completely different. He was wearing shorts, a t-shirt, and sports shoes. The common part was, he was still holding a water bottle in his hand. He greeted Daniel and Dev and sat on the chair next to Daniel.

Daniel called the barman and ordered drinks. Jason asked for Beer, Daniel opted for Whiskey and Dev asked the barman to make sweet lemon juice for him with no ice to be put on that. The barman kept a bowl of cashews, peanuts on the table. The nuts were much bolder and large than Dev has seen in India.

While Dev started eating the nuts, Jason said "today the meeting went well. I think we make get additional work than it was submitted in the first document".

"Yes, the meeting went well, but we have to wait for tomorrow's meeting when the Minister takes any decision. As Director is the in-charge of the project and project funds, he should be able to convince the minister. My personal feeling and interpretation from the telephone call with the Director are that we may be asked to submit the proposal again with an increased scope of work and off-course increase budget also." Daniel said cheers and raised the glass.

"I think Dev you should get into consulting," Jason said to Dev.

"Why do you think so Mr. Jason" responded Dev.

"You have most of the qualities of being a consultant or I can say you have qualities of doing consulting works. Technically you were able to understand the need of the client and suggest a possible solution. Secondly, with your friendly way of talking, you were able to befriend the Director and his team". Jason said to Dev.

"What I could see in you are a team player and a strong technical skilled person" Daniel added to Jason. "This I could find from my team, Ayana and Samuel. They were delighted with the technical and friendly conversation you had with them on your first day. Samuel is a young guy and he mentioned that he would like to learn some geospatial techniques from you being in the project."

The moment of realization and the evolution of an expert.

This was the first time when Dev realized his potential. He was been told many times earlier about his qualities as a team player, technical skills. But they were all in his annual review meetings. But on this day, it was a live project meeting outcome, when a client and an experienced consultant speaking about his qualities.

Daniel called for another round of drinks. This time, Daniel asks Dev to take Wine and join them. But Dev chose to go for mixed fruit juice. All three of them continued their discussion for another half an hour and third round of drinks followed by this they had dinner. By 9 PM they finished, and Daniel left for his residence.

Dev went to his room still thinking about the words said by Daniel and Jason about consulting.

The next day Ayana and Samuel were in the hotel at 8:30 AM to receive Dev and Jason. Dev was in the lobby waiting. He saw Ayana, greeted her with the same half hug, and appreciated her for looking gorgeous. This day Ayana was looking super awesome. She was wearing a short red skirt, a red top with a black leather jacket, and black leather high-heel shoe. Ayana also appreciated Dev's presentation of the day before. From the hotel, they all went straight to the Minister's office where Daniel was waiting with the Director. The meeting with Minister went well. It was a short meeting, where the Minister appreciated the team's understanding of the project as was explained by the Director. He asked the team to immediately work on the proposal and submit it in two weeks.

Daniel thanked the minister took permission to leave. He along with Jason, Dev, Ayana, and Samuel went to the Director's office to take an official letter. Director has already prepared the letter in the name of Daniel's company, requesting them to resubmit the proposal with the revised scope of work, project schedule, and budget. After coming out of the Director's office, he shook hands with all congratulating the team. He said, "We competed till yesterday with five other companies. Today we are the only shortlisted company and added to that we are been asked to submit our proposal again with an increased budget. Now it is going to be a big-budget long term project. Thanks, Dev, Director is happy with you. I hope we are not over committing anything".

"Not to worry Daniel. We can do it. I will make the best team of experts for the project and we will execute it well. I will rain your team in GIS applications for agriculture. I am also glad that I will get more chances of visits to Ethiopia and to be with your team". Responded Dev.

Jason took leave from all. He shook hands with all. He said to Dev to be in touch over email. Jason returned to Netherland the second day after the minister's meeting was over. Daniel requested Samuel and Ayana to take Dev for the lunch in a restaurant to treat with local Ethiopian food so that he (Daniel) can take Jason to the airport. Post lunch, Dev requested for visiting Agriculture university. Ayana took Dev to the Agriculture University where she introduced him as a Geospatial Agriculture Expert with three agriculture lecturers who were going to be part of the project on field survey and data collection. Dev told them that, once the project is finalized, he will work with them and prepare the satellite image-based field survey plan for the project.

This was the second time when Dev started realizing that he has the potential to teach and train others on whatever he has gained through his twelve years of work experience.

Dev spent one additional day in Ethiopia. On the third day of Dev's stay, Dev along with Ayana prepared the new methodology, project schedule, team structure, roles & responsibilities of partner organizations for the project proposal. This was an input for Ayana to start preparing the document. Dev promised to share the detailed technical document once he is back in India and share a meeting update with his business unit head.

Back in India

Dev reported back to the office and explained the meeting to his seniors. Like any other corporate the revised proposal preparation work was assigned to the bidding team and Dev was immediately put into the task with a deadline given by the bidding team for a technical writeup, team preparation, finding external consultants and experts, getting their CVs, and so on. He was never appreciated for the work he did in Ethiopia. He was used to it as this was not the first time.

In this similar situation where most people start blaming the company, bosses and start looking for a new job. They start negotiating with the work they are assigned to. Some of them succeed to get a job in another company. They will end up doing the same work to prove their capabilities.

Dev took this as a learning opportunity and completed the task on time and shared all necessary documents. The bid was submitted to the Ethiopian company. It was confirmed by Daniel's company that the final compiled document with inputs from the Indian team, Jason, and the Agriculture University of Ethiopia is submitted to the end client.

> *"Continuous effort – not strength or intelligence – is the key to unlocking our potential."*
>
> **– Winston Churchill**

Two weeks later, Dev's company received the work order from the Ethiopian company. The project value increased from less than a hundred thousand dollars to close to a million-dollar. The duration of the project increased from twenty-four weeks to three years of the project. And the team from a few GIS executives to experts and consultants working on the project. Dev was given a role to lead the team and to be the client's point of contact. Dev's friends and colleagues praised his work to get a big project for the team and making the team engaged for the next couple of years in an international project. The team planned for a team meeting where they can give a party to Dev unofficially. One of the senior members from Dev's team asked "why don't you become a consultant? You are the "leading light" of the group. After listening to your Ethiopian incidence, you identified the client's problem and understood the need for the project. Then you provided a solution and left it on them to decide. This made the client rethink the project and we all got benefited from a large value project.

From that day onwards Dev shifted his thinking from skill-based project execution to consulting mindset or attitude. He then decided to meet his mentor and learn more about consulting.

This is a narrative of most of the GIS professionals, who spend a major part of their time in the planning of resources and time for the project on how to execute and deliver. Whereas if they realize their strength and start thinking about why the client needs this, how can results help them, how can the project be scaled-up, how can our solution help clients by reducing their cost and increase profitability, then there will not be any feedbacks or repetition of works. They can become a trusted consultant in their domain.

"There is no heavier burden than an unfulfilled potential."

– Charles Schulz

Chapter 2

Transformation of Skillset to Consulting Mindset

"Mindset is more powerful than Skillset."

– Mohd Imteyaz Shaikh

To be a consultant or expert is all about responsibility to solve the problem of clients and transform them from their current state to the desired improved state. To become a consultant once must come out of two main scenarios. One is "Not my job" and the second is "Follow the rule". These two things kill the organization and kill the creativity of an individual. The world is hyper-competitive, and we cannot restrict ourselves to one job and follow the factory-like rules doing one step after the next. There is one more factor that does not allow the mindset to shift. They doubt their expertise, they blame the political situation, etc. Whereas the actual reason is either "I cannot" or "I do not want to"

Dev took a day off from the office to meet his friend who is senior to him in the industry and is also a mentor to him.

Dr. Priya, who is in the GIS industry for about twenty-five years now. Nine years ago, when Dev met Dr. Priya, she has then completed about sixteen years in the industry and was providing consulting support to some of the companies. Although she is from a different domain but has expertise in geospatial technology. She was then a consultant to a mid-size corporate, advisor to two startups and she conducts training for college students.

Dev called her and fixed up a meeting at a Shopping Mall which is in Banjara Hills, Hyderabad. This is a centrally located place in Hyderabad, which is well connected from all places having the best of shopping malls, corporate offices, and residence of high-profile businessmen, movie personalities, and political backgrounds. Dev selected this place as this shopping mall has a dedicated floor for the meetings, food, and drinks section. In this section, one corner which is about 20% of the floor area, has the food counters, and the remaining 80% of the area is kept for guests to sit, discuss, and enjoy food.

The day of the meeting was decided on Friday so that the weekend is not spoiled. Also, there will be fewer crowds during office hours. Dev wanted to have complete clarity and hence he decided on a full-day meeting. Dev reached the place well before the decided time of 10 AM and reserved the seat close to the glass wall. The restaurant was on the fifth floor and the glass wall faces outside towards the road and market lane. Dev sat there looking at the busy road with vehicles from the top.

After about five minutes, Dr. Priya joined Dev at the restaurant. She was looking beautiful in her grey color salwar suit with a purple border, she left her hair open and was wearing frameless spectacles. She was holding a diary, a cardholding purse, and two cellphones. She came from the back and gave a pat on Dev's back. Dev got up from the chair and greeted her with a handshake. Both have a friend cum mentor-mentee relationship. She started asking about Dev's family, his trip to Ethiopia, and his office work. Dev explained everything that happened in Ethiopia and his office.

Dev asked Dr. Priya.

"Can I become a consultant? Can I get into consulting? I only have ten years of experience. I do not have a Ph.D. in my subject and not many international papers are published. I agree that I am good at my subject and have skills in GIS and remote sensing. I have been successful in project execution and client interaction. I am also good at technical documentation and technical marketing. Does that mean, I can become a consultant"? Dev questions Dr. Priya.

"I can understand the doubt you are carrying in your mind. You do not need to be a grey-haired man with bundles of certificates and dozens of publications to become a consultant. These are all myths that most of the professionals are having". Responded Dr. Priya

"Let us get some coffee and snacks so that we can spend quality time on learning consulting". Dr. Priya told to Dev.

Dev gets up immediately and requests her to be in the seat otherwise someone else may occupy the seat if they found it vacant. Dev rushes towards the food counter to get coffee, French fries, and some cookies for both.

Dr. Priya started explaining to Dev.

"Dev, I know you for the past many years. You have the best technical skills in your subject. You work hard and with dedication on any assignment that is given to you. Your team likes you and they treat you as your leader. I know you like a nice humble person and a good friend of mine".

"As I told you earlier that you do not need to wait for your hairs to turn grey, get multiple qualifications, and all to become a consultant. I know your hairs are not going to turn grey at all as you will become bald in a couple of years." She makes fun of him and continues.

A simple definition of consulting is "providing professional or expert advice".

Consulting can be defined as an act of providing expert knowledge to a third party for a fee. Consulting is most often used when a company needs an outside, expert opinion regarding a business decision.

"Consulting is more like a generalist, whereas with the specific domain it becomes expert consulting. Let me put the definition to your domain". Said, Dr. Priya

Agriculture consulting can be defined as providing expert subject-specific knowledge to an organization working in agribusiness activities. For example, Agrochemical Industry requires expert advice from agronomists, Entomologists, and meteorologists. Similarly, agriculture commodity trading groups may require expert advice from agronomists, agribusiness professionals, and agriculture technology professionals.

"And to define further with your subject and skillset that makes you even more specialized, then we can define *Geospatial Agriculture Consulting* as an act of providing services to key stakeholders in agriculture using the latest advanced tools and technology such as remote sensing (RS), geographic information system (GIS), a global positioning system (GPS). The main objective of this consulting is to increase sales or productivity and to decrease costs for clients. The key interested party can be a geospatial service providing company or the agribusiness sector".

Becoming an expert/consultant in geospatial agriculture is the best way to create the maximum amount of success in agribusiness. As a consultant, you will be greatly appreciated by your clients or colleagues. One cannot become an expert at anything that you do not know or understand. One must gain the most amount of knowledge that you can learn. The more you educate yourself, the more that you will be able to authentically promote yourself as the leading authority.

"It is like medical doctors of different expertise. If I get a toothache, I will not go to an Eye specialist, rather I will take the services of a

Dentist. So, a Dentist is like a dental consultant providing services to patients having dental problems. Similarly, if my house has an electrical problem, then I will call an electrician and not the plumber. They can be young or old, it does not matter but they should have expertise and experience in solving problems. In the geospatial sector, the generalists are commonly addressed as GIS Executives and specialists are addressed as GIS Specialists". Dev responded to Dr. Priya.

It was already two hours spent. Dev went to the food counter to get snacks. This time, he gets "Mirchi Pakoda" and "Samosa". Mirchi Pakora is a fried snack (fritter) prepared from big and bold green chili, originating from the Indian subcontinent. It is a popular snack across the Indian subcontinent, where it is served in restaurants and sold by street vendors. These are less spicy than usual chili. And Samosa is a small triangular pastry filled with spiced meat or vegetables and fried in ghee or oil.

"You got a broad idea about consulting. And you know Dev, there are many types of consultants in the industry. These are generally an expert or an experienced professional in a specific field and have a wide knowledge of the subject. He/She is a professional who provides expert advice in a specific area such as, business, education, law, human resources, marketing, finance, health care, engineering, science, or any of many other specialized fields" Dr. Priya continued her talk explaining Dev about types on consultants and types of the consulting role an individual can play.

It has been a long time we are sitting here. Let us go out and discuss more on this. They came down to the ground floor which was a children's play area. Few families were present with their kids playing around. They spotted an empty bench colored in red, blue, and yellow color. It had a large-sized umbrella for shade, kept by some company for their advertisement. An air cooler next to the seat was making the place more comfortable.

Dr. Priya resumed her discussion and stated to Dev.

As of today, we have many individuals like Dev in Geospatial Industry who are working as GIS Engineers, GIS Executive, GIS Manager, GIS Specialist, RS Analyst, and many other similar designations. These individuals are highly skilled and work very effectively to execute the project on time. They are delivery oriented. I would like to make a point here that a change in shift of mindset or attitude for these individuals is required. Professionals, who are working in Agriculture projects should think of any project with a purpose to meet the client's needs and with a purpose to solve the problem that the client is facing. Hence for this, one must think and act like a consultant- a problem solver.

You might have heard about the most common types of consultants such as Business consultants; Sales consultants; Marketing consultants; Accounting consultants; Technology (IT) consultants; Legal consultants; Public relations consultants. These are experts in their subject but can be fitted into any industry. For example, a marketing consultant can be a consultant to phone making company and also to fertilizer making company. His/her role is to define the marketing strategy for the company's product (whatever the product maybe).

In the Indian Agriculture sector generally, a consultant refers to a retired person/grey-haired aged individual, who has spent his life in a subject either in the government department or in a private company. For example, crop experts, soil experts, plant protection specialists, etc. They become part of a project to provide the solution to the problems faced by any organization. In the same organization, any young, experienced professionals will be often called a "Subject Matter Expert" (SME) such as SME-crop, SME-plant protection, SME-soil, SME-horticulture, SME-Agri-Engineering, etc. They have attained knowledge in respective subjects, and they provide their expertise in the domain as per the requirement of the project. These agriculture experts are rarely called consultants.

The need is to have a shift in the mindset. If the expert gets into consulting in Agriculture, then these common consulting can be renamed as

- Agribusiness consultant – Helps in the growth and management of the agriculture business of a company.

- Agri Commodity Sales consultant – Helps in teambuilding for product sales and developing strategy for Agri commodity sales.

- Agriculture Marketing consultant – Helps in branding and lead generation.

- Agribusiness Accounting consultant – Helps in finance management of agribusiness company such as budgeting, cash flow analysis, and P&L of company.

- Agribusiness Legal consultant – Helps in legal matters such as agreements and partnerships of agriculture companies.

- Farmer Training consultant – Helps in strategizing and coordinating the training and demonstration in the field.

- Agri-Tech consultant – Helps the research and development department in the company's R&D activities such as the development of new varieties, restructuring of the composition of fertilizers of protective chemicals, use of digital tools during field surveys and demonstrations, etc.

Dev was silently listening to her and observing the fluency and confidence she had in her talk. She had an incredibly unique way of explaining which Dev has observed for the past many years. She will always carry a notepad and pen. Her explanation would be by scribbling on the paper making it simpler for the listener. One of the charts from her notes is given here.

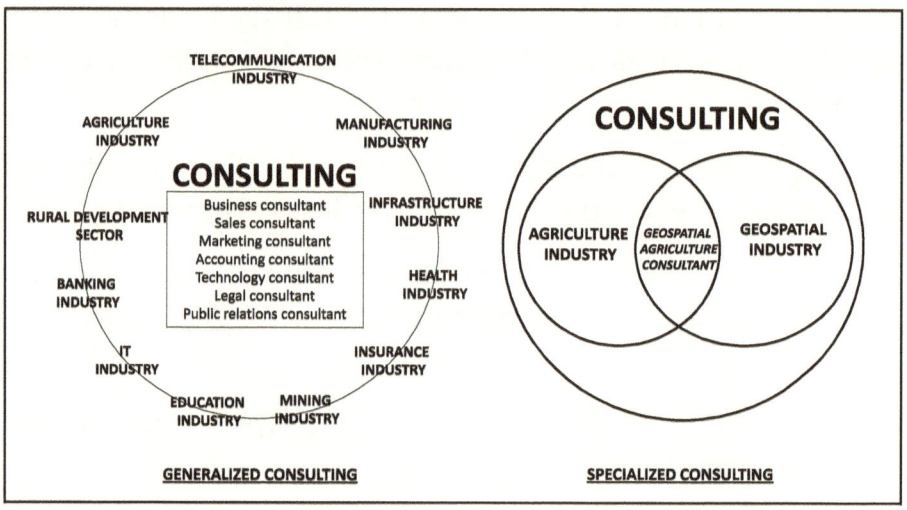

She continued her talk. "Now let us consider an expert like you (Dev). You are an expert as I described earlier, but you have an additional specialized skill of using geospatial techniques for solving the problem. Hence you are a Geospatial Agriculture Consultant". An individual who helps in solving the problem of an Agriculture organization using geospatial technology with the purpose to reduce cost and increase productivity or profitability can be called a *Geospatial Agriculture Consultant.*

Dr. Priya drew to diagrams and said, *"These diagrams can illustrate this more clearly".*

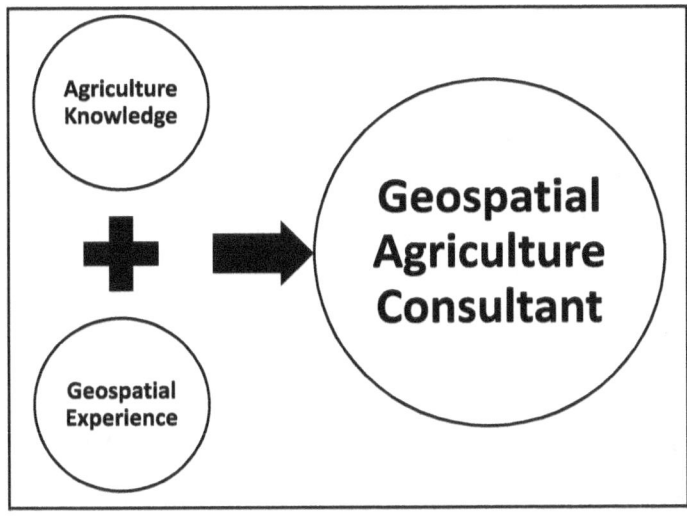

- He/she can be an agriculture professional with experience of working using geospatial technology OR
- He/she can be a geoinformatics professional having experience in agriculture-based projects.

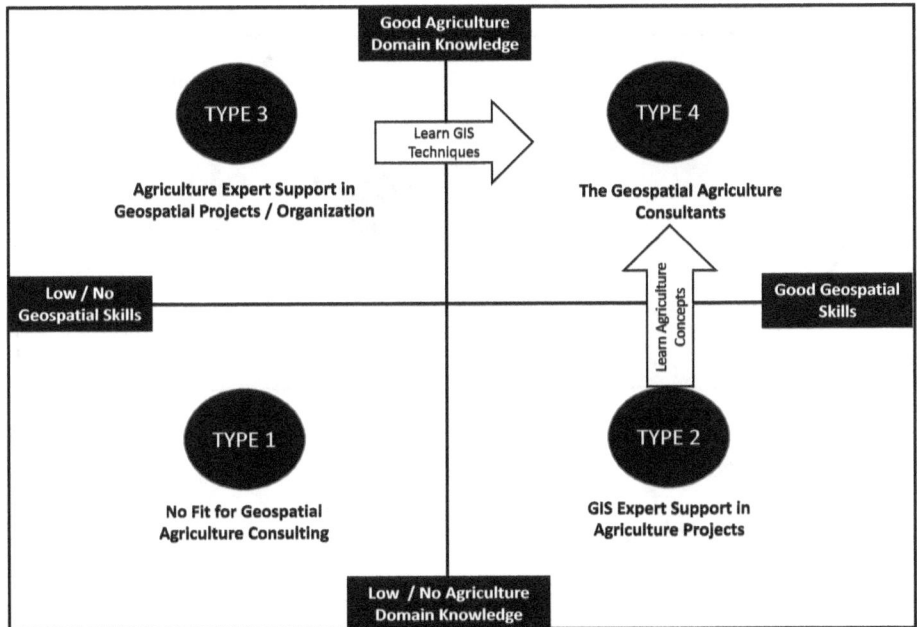

Dev cited to Dr. Priya, "As I understand from your description, with the expertise and experience I have gained over by working in Agriculture projects using GIS and remote sensing techniques, I have the potential to become a consultant or say, I can get into Geospatial Agriculture consulting. But do I need to resign from my job? I have heard that, consultants do not have a boss and they work as and when they feel like".

Dr. Priya interrupted Dev and said. "These are myths Dev. Now let me make clear some questions for you".

The first question is, when and why does anyone hire a consultant?

The answer to this is an organization that wants to achieve something for which they need help from a person who has skills to attain that or who has experience in that area. They know their current state and know what their desired state is, but they do not know how to reach there. For this, they need the advice to get there. This is where the consultants play important role in an organization or an individual's growth.

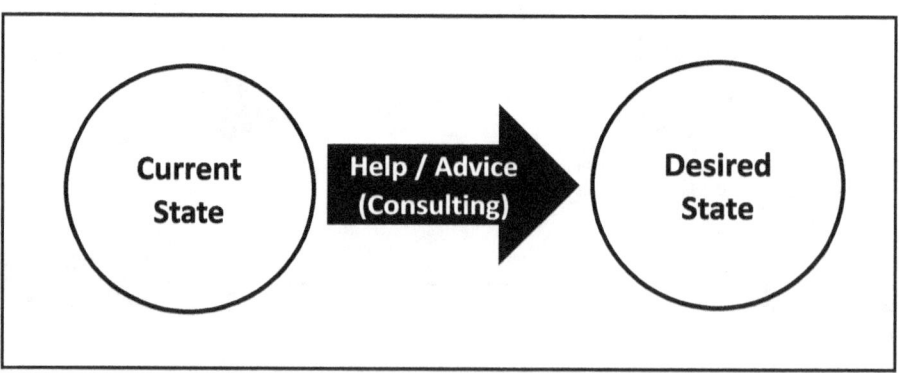

Hence, consulting can be defined in a simple term as

- *helping people solve problems and achieve results.*
- *helping an organization solve problems and achieve results.*

- *helping the project team solve problems and achieve results.*
- *helping business units solve problems and achieve results.*

The second question is, how do Geospatial Agriculture Consultants work?

The role of Geospatial Agriculture consultant can fall under one of two general categories:

- Internal consultant: someone who operates within an organization but is available to be consulted on areas of their specialization by other departments.
- External consultant: someone who is employed externally to the client whose expertise is provided temporarily, usually for a fee.

The third question is, what are the reasons for engaging Geospatial Agriculture Consultants?

There could be many reasons to hire a consultant or to get advice from outside:

1. They know where to go but have no idea of how to go.
2. They want to reach their desired state earlier than thought.
3. They know that they cannot reach their goal on their own.
4. They would like to believe and use an established approach by a skilled person.

("They" can be referred to GIS companies, Government departments, NGOs implementing developmental projects, Agriculture companies generating Agriculture intelligence information, etc.)

"I will take leave for now and you think about these questions. Tomorrow is off day for me, so we will meet again and discuss the myths of consulting", said Dr. Priya.

"Sure Dr. Priya and thank you for your time today. It was good learning for me. We will meet again tomorrow", stated Dev and both started walking towards the parking area.

Dev had some clarity now. His dream of providing service to others, giving training, and helping others through his learnings were getting directions. Dev realized that these can be achieved through the consulting approach. He went home, spent a good time with his family, and was relaxed.

> *"Once your mindset changes, everything on the outside will change along with it."*
>
> – **Steve Maraboli**

Chapter 3

Nine Myths of Consulting

"Myths and science fulfill a similar function: they both provide human beings with a representation of the world and of the forces that are supposed to govern it. They both fix the limits of what is considered as possible"

– François Jacob

On the second day of learning sessions, it was decided to meet at Dr. Priya's office. Her office was made in terrace portico. The walls and interiors were very professionally made. She has also converted another room for conducting small-group training sessions. Dev reached the meeting place at the decided time of 9:30 AM. He greeted Dr. Priya with a smile and a handshake at the entrance gate. She was in her casual dress, wearing blue jeans and kurta (A loose collarless shirt worn by people from South Asia, usually with a salwar, churidars, or pant). She had her hair tied like a pony, with her spectacles on. She wore a sandal that was neither flat nor high heels and made a nice sound when they started climbing stairs. She has converted the top floor of her home into an office and a training room. It is a small office, where three to four guests can comfortably sit. A medium-sized table is placed in the corner where she sits and does her work. The table was neat and clean, with a laptop placed in the center, a cardholder, and a pen-stand on the right side, her diary, and pen on the left side of the table. There was a whiteboard on the other corner of the room. The room had a connecting door leading to another room which was meant for training. She asked

Dev to sit comfortably and went downstairs to get some juice and snacks. Within few minutes she was back with two cups of coffee, a plate filled with cookies, another plate with cut fruits, a jar full of mango juice, and a bottle of water.

"We should not get disturbed in between our discussion, hence I got all these". She said to Dev while passing over the coffee cup to him. She went to the whiteboard and wrote on top "Myths of Consulting" and also the date of discussion.

By taking a sip of coffee, she told "Dev, there is a lot of misconception among people about the lifestyle of consultants. Even I had these doubts a couple of years back. Now I have learned and realized after getting into the consulting profession. Today in this meeting, we will discuss some common myths of becoming a consultant. Once these myths are cleared it will be easy for you to start working on your steps to become a consultant".

Especially in the agriculture sector, there is a common belief in our mind that a consultant is a grey-haired man with more than 25 to 30 years of experience in the industry, retired, professional having doctorate (Ph.D.), must have more than dozens of research publications on his name, written or contributed in books and guided research students in his career. It is also believed that consultant has a lot of money, who spend few hours giving advice and take lots of money, consultants travel a lot and all his expenses are taken care of by his client and he is been paid hefty.

These are all not completely true. These can also be termed as "*Self-limiting beliefs*". In the present day business environment, consultants are hired based on individuals' skills. Three main qualities are looked in to hire him/her as a consultant. These are-

- Competencies
- Capabilities
- Capacities

Let us understand these qualities.

Competencies: This is the ability of an individual to utilize a skill or ability to use a tool. For example, a person having skills in handling RS/GIS software where data coming from the field can be analyzed and results can be generated in the form of reports that can help in planning and decision making. In such a case he can be considered as a consultant for database analysis.

Capabilities: This is the ability to use the skills at the right time, in the right way, and in the right place. For example, a person has skills of using the tools but if he analyzed the results and gives a report when the season is over then it if will be of no use for any planning or decision making. Hence along with competencies, an individual should have the capability to use the tools in the right way and produce the results at right time.

Capacities: This is an individual's quality of handling the situation. He should have flexibility, soft, imaginative, team player. These qualities reflect his conduct more than his method of doing work.

Once an individual has all these qualities along with the required qualification and certifications then he/she is fit to be called a consultant.

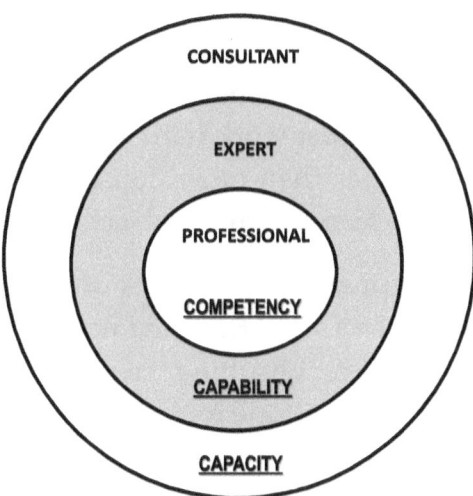

While sipping tea and having cookies, Dr. Priya stated, "based on our last evening discussion, I found that there are some myths about consulting. We will be discussing some important of them. I have NINE of them selected which will cover most of the doubts. She wrote on top as *"Nine myths of Consulting"* on top of the whiteboard and started explaining one after the other.

Myth No. 1: "No Boss, Free Bird"

This is a common belief that consultants are a free bird and they do not have any boss to report to. This is not always true. A consultant reports to all his/her customers and clients. Even sometimes, the client team in which he is part of takes a report of the consultant's work. The good part is, no one monitors a consultant administratively but his timings, breaks taken in a day, dressing, attendance, etc. A consultant must have his discipline.

A consultant is not always a free bird but is bound by the timeline of project delivery. Some projects require a lot of extra hours of work. Yes, the truth in this is, a consultant can choose his time and comfortable place of work. He can be or he can choose to be a free bird when he is not having any consulting assignment.

Myth No. 2: "No Hard work"

There is a misbelief that Consultants do not have to work hard. This is not true. Consultants must work hard to be in the market, to be updated, and to be better than other consultants in competition. Consultants must keep learning their subject.

In consulting, change projects and clients often, you may have to work late hours, it will be a short term and not the norm throughout your consulting career. Yes, consulting is a work-hard environment, but not as bad as the myths allude to.

In the agriculture sector, there are a lot of new things happening. New pests, new diseases, changes in cropping pattern, the impact of climate change. Similarly, in the geospatial sector, new software and applications, different models for different crops, different project locations, etc. For example, some clients chose to work in paid software, and some chose for open source. Hence one has to work hard to keep updating and keep learning new things to be able to provide the best solution to the client.

Myth No. 3: "Grey Hair, long years of experience, publications"

Consultants need to be experts as specialists and have many years of experience. This is partially true. Yes, a geospatial agriculture consultant needs to be an expert in GIS and Remote Sensing and should understand Agriculture. He can also be an expert in Agriculture and working knowledge of GIS and Remote Sensing.

He should have the required skills to understand and solve the problem of a customer. This expertise can come from few years of working experience. One need not require many long years of experience to be called a consultant.

Myth No. 4: "Remote work and are Disconnected"

Another common worry about hiring independent consultants, especially for remote work, is that they will be too disconnected from your day-to-day operations and the rest of your team. However, with the advent of so many online and cloud-based tools for GIS and Image processing, data sharing options, real-time video communications, and screen sharing facilities, remote workers are nearly as connected as traditional employees.

While working together in the same place offers some unique advantages when you are a training consultant or when you are working with an inexperienced team. It can also create disadvantages such as lost productivity office meetings, and distractions from noise, phone calls, and other interruptions.

Myth No. 5: "Immune to office politics"

Office politics is a part of the work environment. People like complainers and gossipers apply strategies to gain advantage or for support to move up the hierarchical ladder or for personal gains. Consultants are not always protected from office politics. Consultants do face office politics. Since there will be a project team for whom the consultant might be working. If any recommendation made by the consultant goes against the team member, then he may get into the trap of office politics. GIS-based agriculture projects are more often a team-based project where field surveyor, image processing expert, analysis expert, and documentation expert reinvolved. A consultant must work in coordination with all. There will be people who hate your knowledge and confidence. There will be people who want to be like you, but they cannot, so they dislike you for who you are. Some employees may even argue that consultants are overpaid to do the same work that they do.

Myth No. 6: "Loaded with projects and clients"

From the outside, it looks that clients line up at the door of consultants, which is not true. A consultant must market himself, create a network to get clients. Getting clients and get projects in your area of expertise is not easy. One must prove his competency, capabilities, and capacity to solve the problem faced by any client (explained in chapter 4). In projects of geospatial application in agriculture, a consultant must identify the needs of the client, create a project out of the need. If he/she can do it alone fine, else must look for a service providing company and become part of them. Yes, multiple projects can line up at a later stage where you have solved problems of multiple clients and have benefited in their business.

At that time with word-of-mouth marketing, consultants get clients on their own.

Myth No. 7: "No Trust"

This is a concern of most companies that one cannot trust a consultant who knows more than you. This situation arises when a consultant adds scope of work and activities. The best example of this is when we face a problem with our car or scooter. The mechanic examines the vehicle and then tells what all things are required to be done. Similarly, when a geospatial agriculture consultant is hired, he/she identifies the problem from the client's point of view and lists the requirements of the project to fulfill the client's needs. If the requirement goes out of the budgeted list, then the client gets feeling that managing an expert is tricky business, for the simple fact that they know more than you.

A good technical consultant will share inside information with you, explaining the risks, the costs, and then give you space to make follow up decisions on your own. Hence the quality of a trusted consulted is, he/she never submits a financial proposal till the scope and deliverables are finalized. Another advantage of a good technical geospatial agriculture consultant is with an area of expertise over a more general consultant, where an expert can build a concrete solution and put technical systems in place to make sure the process will be carried effortlessly.

Myth No. 8: "Significant funds and spending on administration"

One of the common myths is that, to begin, you need to have significant funds to build an office, create marketing materials, and spend a large number of fees on lawyers, accountants, and administration. This is not in all cases. One can start on his own, from his home with a little cash. A good skill, reputation, and a healthy professional network are the basic requirements of an independent consultancy.

Though having some basic promotion in place is beneficial. The more money you have in savings the better off you will be in the long-term, but you do not need to spend a lot of funds upfront to get started. Working from home has become so commonplace in business today, no one will worry about it.

Myth No. 9: "Easy scaling and expansion"

People say, scaling up and expanding of consulting business is quite easy. Scaling is an indicator of your past performance and successes you had. Another myth is with more money it is easy to expand. As we know agriculture consulting is not selling but is more of a relationship building. Scaling and expansion require a mindset shift from being a solo technical expert to become an entrepreneur running consulting form. This learning will be required on hiring the best talent or training the team at the same level of expertise and automate the processes and systems. At times for scaling, you may have to leave part of your earnings by outsourcing side activities while focusing on core business. Since consulting is more on relations and trust, the same qualities need to be built in team members.

When a consultant is growing a business, it's easy to become distracted by new people, opportunities, and ideas. You might offer a consulting service to make some cash today, even though you know it will not scale. Or you might make the mistake of diving into a new business opportunity that is completely unrelated to your domain. This can happen when geospatial agriculture consultants are not having many agriculture projects and will try to jump into any GIS-based projects.

Dr. Priya said to Dev, "before you think of scaling a consulting business, ask yourself why. For instance, a consultant who can earn enough to provide for his idea and skills without working many hours may not need to scale his business. Instead of scaling up, the right path for him maybe to keep his business small, lean, and easily manageable. I am in this category. This is giving me a good work-family balance time".

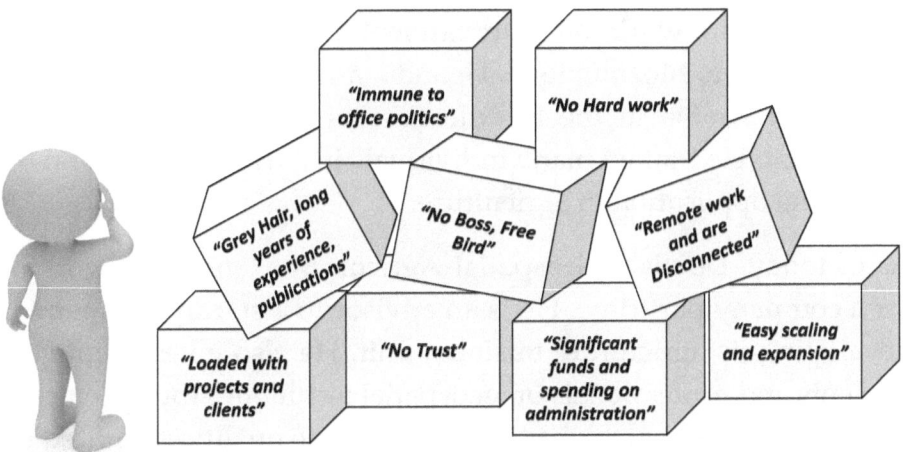

There is another myth that says that consultants get stuck with bad customers. This usually happens when you over the project and underdeliver. Consultants have the benefit to fire a bad customer. This comes with a risk of losing a client and payment.

It was about Noon and by this time both had finished coffee, snacks, and juices. In between, Dr. Priya explained the myths with examples of companies she worked with and the experience she got from other consulting friends and some from her own experience.

Dev had series of meetings with Dr. Priya. Where she clarified the myths, the different types of consulting roles, and consulting business. She introduced Dev to some of the other consultants in the industry to understand the role they are playing for the client. She took Dev to few companies and introduced him to top management so that Dev can get an idea of why companies need a consultant.

Dev learned a lot from Dr. Priya, other consultants, business owners, and scientists from research organizations. Dev continued with his job and started working on the qualities required for consulting. He completed his master's in business management and did few technical certificate courses. During this period, he changed his approach to helping others and solving problems. Dev got the opportunity to work on international projects. He traveled to Malawi, Kenya, Mozambique, Uganda, and Sierra Leone in Africa, and Saudi Arabia in the Middle East as Geospatial Agriculture Consultant. He trained many individuals in Africa and India on the geospatial application in agriculture.

As of today, Dev is a Geospatial Agriculture Consultant working for a company part-time. He is an advisor to a startup company in developing its agriculture business unit. He also gives training to students and professionals on geospatial techniques for agriculture. In the next few chapters, he teaches about the qualities required for a consultant, consultative selling approaches, and steps to become a consultant.

> *[In refutation of evolution] You know what, evolution is a myth. … Why aren't monkeys still evolving into humans?*
>
> *– **Christine O'Donnell***

Section 2

Uncover

Recognize <u>Uncover</u> Learn Engage Secure

Chapter 4

Nine Specific Skills of Geospatial Consultant

Success is not only measured by money. One can also be rich by his habits, values, vision, and discipline.

As an expert or a consultant, to be preferred by a customer, you must present yourself in a way that they believe you can do what you say you can do. An expert must make the impression with the knowledge s/he carries and the way s/he treats others. There is never a second chance for an expert to make a first impression.

A geospatial agriculture expert (consultant) is always in the business of solving customer's problems. If he cannot understand the problem or the requirement, how can the customer trust the expert to get his job done? S/he is a brand by itself, that connects a bunch of elements viz. how you present yourself, how you treat others, what you know, what you do, how you take others along.

Most of the experts in the geospatial sector are the best in their technical skills. They work hard and give their best in the project. You will agree to it, and most of you would have felt that despite doing the hard work, finding the solution for the complicated tasks, and spending extra time in every project, you are undervalued, unappreciated, or unseen.

The reason for this with the GIS expert is, s/he always keeps oneself competing with the person next to him or her and keep practicing the known technique. This is because of the fear of getting replaced. These talented experts, unfortunately, do not take extra time to work on learning new techniques and on their soft skills. To be a trusted expert or a leading light, you need to have a combination of technical and soft skills.

For a consultant in geospatial agriculture, there is an additional third skill required, which is consulting skills. The first being technical skills, which is the expertise in agriculture, remote sensing, and GIS technology. This preferably is beyond what is been learned in college. This is the expertise gained by working on customer projects. The second skill is soft skills or interpersonal skills that include the way of working with people. This needs your ability to articulate your conceptual thinking into words, listening to others, and supporting the team members. The third skill is the consulting skill, which includes the approach designing from identifying customer need to providing the solution.

This creates a personal brand and differentiates you from everyone else and raise you above others in your field, in your niche, and your industry. This also encourages clients to choose you not because of your skills or expertise but also because of who you are.

> *"Technical skills may get you a job, but soft skills can either make you or break you as a leader"*

The Trusted Geospatial Agriculture Consultant - Separate from the crowd.

The goal of a consultant is to be accepted as a "trusted consultant", or as a "leading light" as this emphasizes the trust that is required in the agriculture business. This can only happen between humans. This level of trust cannot be developed between humans and machines. One must have certain qualities to succeed in consulting. In agriculture, trust is the most important currency in the value chain such as the trust between seed supplier and farmers on quality, the trust between farmer and bank on money (loan), trust between farmer and agriculture officer on new technology, trust between farmer and buyer on farm produce, trust between the processor and consumer and so on.

Correspondingly, in the Geospatial sector, trust plays an overly critical role. An agriculture expert with geospatial skills can understand the problem of the client and suggest the best possible solution where they can save the cost. In the geospatial sector, there is a dependency on third party inputs such as satellite images and field survey. Hence a consultant can be the best judge to suggest the type of images that can serve the purpose of the project. However, if there is trust in the ability and integrity, clients will work with these consultants to get their problems solved.

> *"Trust has to be earned, and should come only after the passage of time."*
>
> – **Arthur Ashe**

Trust is not any subject to be learned and byhearted, neither is any product that can be purchased. Whereas it must be earned and should come only over time with practice and habit. We spend our time and energy trying to perfect our craft (image processing, GIS, AI/ML, agronomy, soils, etc.), but we do not focus on the skills and interactions that will allow us to stand out and become the "leading light" to our organization.

If you have a strong belief in the ability, reliability, integrity of someone, then it means that you have trust in him. Being a geospatial agriculture consultant, your team members, your vendors, and your customers should have confidence in your honesty and integrity. This will lead to building trust and belief that this expert will do the things he says he can.

In this section, the best-required qualities are explained that a consultant needs to possess. We all have these qualities. We need to uncover it. Some of these may require learning, some may need practice and some implementation. Once again, we will go with the number Nine and the top nine skills/qualities which is particularly essential for a trusted consultant to have.

Skill No. 1: Expert Knowledge or Specialized Knowledge

There are two types of knowledge. One that is obtained as part of our schooling in schools and colleges. The second is the knowledge gained with experience. In the geospatial agriculture sector, knowledge is one of the most important assets or qualities that one must have to be called as an expert or a consultant. And this knowledge must be a combination of both that is learned in colleges and that is gained with working experience.

An individual who has a basic certification or graduation in Agriculture and has been applying remote sensing and GIS technique in agriculture projects for years and years is the best fit to be a geospatial agriculture consultant. The other best category of individuals is those who have certifications or graduation in geoinformatics and have been applying GIS and remote sensing techniques in agriculture projects over years are also the best fit to be Geospatial Agriculture Consultant.

The basic technical skills that are required in geospatial agriculture consulting can be broadly categorized into the following.

- Agriculture Subject Knowledge – A basic understanding of the subject is very much essential for executing any geospatial agriculture projects. Some of the specific areas are Crop information, agronomy, soil science, climatic condition for agriculture, geography, landscape, soil-scape, water, irrigation, etc. This helps in the selection of correct input for the project. A simple mistake on an incorrect selection of satellite images can lead to a project disaster. For example, the season and month of images are critical for crop and soil-related studies. Similarly, understanding of crop, its stages, its growing pattern, its life cycle from sowing till harvesting is also very essential for crop-related projects. Basic awareness about the soil is also necessary. This helps in identifying the type of crop that is suitable for a specific type of soil. Also, to differentiate among the same type of crop between two different types of soil. Soil and its properties help in managing irrigation and watershed related projects. It has been observed that a lot of companies ignore this and get into project failure. This leads to bringing down the confidence of the client in geospatial technology.

- Fundamentals of Remote Sensing and Geographic Information System: This is another particularly important subject that is required for a consultant to learn. He should have expertise in basic techniques such as Image processing, interpretation, classification, and analysis technique. The definition of GIS tells the complete need of it. Geographic Information System (GIS) is an integrated, spatial, data-handling program that will collect, store, and retrieve spatial data from the real world. These are powerful tools in analysis and decision-making. This is linked with the processing work that is taking place in the image as a raster or vector format. In simple terms, GIS helps in analyzing, storing, and presenting it to the customer/user.

- Reporting and documentation technique – This is the quality like toppings on the cake. Once the technical stuff is done, it must be reported, documented, and to be presented to the customer. Geospatial technology is science as well as art. The art of presenting your results. There is an art in doing the task which will be covered in subsequent qualities. A geospatial agriculture consultant needs to be creative in executing the project.

- Market knowledge – to be trusted by a client as an expert, the knowledge of the market and updated technology is essential. In the geospatial agriculture sector, updated knowledge about agriculture and the latest information about the geospatial industry can make you more qualified to be a trusted consultant.

The discomfort

It has been now five decades since when the first project on remote sensing was used in agriculture. Robert B. Macdonald, National Aeronautics and Space Administration, Lyndon B. Johnson Space Center, Houston, in their article *"A summary of the history of the development of automated remote sensing for agricultural applications"* published in IEEE Transactions on Geoscience and Remote Sensing (Volume: GE-22, Issue: 6, Nov. 1984) stated that *"In 1970, an airborne MSS was used in the Corn Blight Watch – the first large-scale application of remote sensing in agriculture. During 1972 and 1973, research established the feasibility of automating digital classification to process high volumes of Landsat MSS data. The Large Area Crop Inventory Experiment (LACIE) successfully demonstrated automated processing of Landsat MSS data in estimating wheat crop production on a global basis"*.

Despite fifty years of geospatial technology application in agriculture, it has still not reached the key players in the agriculture value chain. The end-users still have very little confidence in this technology. When we meet them, they raise the following types of questions.

"Can GIS and RS solve the problem of getting information on crop acreage health and yield?"

"How accurate will be the information?"

"How reliable will be the results?"

"Can soil base study such as soil fertility assessment be done using this technology?"

"Can irrigation planning or water resources management be done by this technology?"

"We will still validate the satellite-based information with our field survey data?"

"Can geospatial technology solution reduce our expenditure of field and increase revenue?"

These queries are fair with the users, but the concern is "why these questions". The research on this technology has moved from hot-air balloon image analysis to aircraft-based photographs, then from low (at kilometer) to very-high spatial resolution satellite images (at centimeter). As of today, even drones are used to generate an image at very-high spatial-resolution and on any selected day.

Is it because the service providers were not able to provide the best solutions? No, the reason is the right people were not using technology, especially in the agriculture sector. If we look at the countries in Asia and Africa, very less agriculture graduates, which will be less than one percent as compared to total agriculture graduates in the world are involved in this. Among these also, the majority are in research and development institutions.

Of late it has been observed that many startup companies have emerged in the agriculture sector. Most of their founders and owners are from the non-agriculture background. These companies have a high preference for digital technology to make digital agriculture products. These companies prefer to hire software application development professionals more than agriculture subject matter experts. The reason for these companies to not succeed in their expectation is for not having subject matter experts especially agriculture experts. Another reason for their slow growth is the wrong assumption about agriculture subject which according to them includes sowing of seed, adding fertilizers, spraying chemicals, harvesting, selling in the market, and repeat the same in successive season/year.

This is the reason most of the GIS-based companies be it big or small, old or new, well established or startup, they are either service providers or solution sellers. They are not called problem solvers.

As a geospatial agriculture consultant, one must first identify the problem, diagnose the problem, design a plan of action, develop a methodology, implement the action, suggest recommendations, and provide a solution to the problem. We will discuss in detail the consulting approach in a later section in this book.

Clients typically look for a consultant for two reasons: 1) expects the consultant to have more expertise than the organization's internal resources or 2) because clients do not have sufficient time to solve their problems or implement their projects. A consultant's level of knowledge should be broad enough to know when to ask questions and/or where to research to find solutions. A consultant should always remain updated by reading research papers, journals, magazines, and through networking with fellow consultants. S/he should know how to apply theory into practice and be skillful in using appropriate tools (software, instruments) to function efficiently in the job.

Skill No. 2: Problem solver

Clients look for consultants who can detect the cause of the problem and provide logical solutions. They are "problem solvers". There are two types of problem solvers. The first one is when the problem is known. This consultant identifies the problem faced by a client, then does the analysis by himself or gets it done by the team and finally delivers results. The second one when the client does not know about the problem. This consultant asks questions in a way that client can identify their problem and then the consultant helps the client in identifying the best solution to solve that problem.

In agriculture, problem-solving is one of the key qualities anyone should acquire if he intends to become an agriculture consultant. If we just rely on the knowledge obtained during schooling or graduation, then it will be easy to work on the task but will be difficult to solve any problem. For this one needs to have specialized knowledge gained with experience. In addition to this one needs to have a tool or skill to identify and solve the problem of customers.

Abraham Maslow said that *"If your only tool is a hammer then every problem looks like a nail."*

Imagine that a patient goes to a doctor and says, "I have a stomachache. I need XYZ (name) medicine. Please prescribe the same and I will collect it from the medicine store".

If the doctor, writes the prescription and provides him the medicine, then he has done the service to the patient but not solved his problem.

In a similar situation if the conversation goes like this……

Patient: "Hello doctor I have a stomachache, I need XYZ (name) medicine. Please prescribe the same and I will collect it from the medicine store".

Doctor: "Sure, I will do that. Please have a seat. Tell me did you hit your body somewhere, or did any object hit your stomach area".

Patient: "No doctor".

Doctor: "Well. That means this is not an external injury or any pain in the muscle or bone. Did you eat any street food or any spicy food recently"?

Patient: "Yes doctor, I had but that's now a long time ago. Maybe more than two weeks from today. It was not spicy but yes we had a party at street food corner".

Doctor: "Okay, we will diagnose that further. There is a little chance of any food poisoning. Tellme, if you have taken water from any unknown sources".

Patient: "Yes doctor, the day before yesterday, I was on a field visit. It was a long distance from the city. While retuning my water in the bottle got over and I took the water from my driver's bottle. I have seen him filling his bottle from the restaurant we had our lunch."

Doctor: "Okay the cause of stomachache is due to the water you had that might be contaminated with germs. And the same water would have been used for lunch preparation. Hence, I will prescribe another set of medicine along with a three-day course of antibiotics. This will cure your stomach problem. In case you still face any problem then give me a call on my number, then I will change the medicine. You need not have to come again to my clinic".

This is where the doctor did the consultation and recommended the right solution to the patient. The patient was also happy in knowing the actual cause of his problem. He will be careful now in the future.

Let us further understand this with one of Dev's consulting experience where agriculture business owner takes the help of geospatial service providing company.

Mr. Vijayan is a maize crop head for the Asia Pacific region in a multinational agriculture commodity trading company. They have their field team in India, and they get field level information from this team. Recently they have expanded their maize procurement from other countries in South East Asia viz., Indonesia, and Bangladesh. They also use government published data to analyze their commodity buying and selling. For these countries, they have a small team that also does field-based information collection about the crop. However, it does not cover the full country. The data obtained from field and data from published sources are analyzed and extrapolated to the country level to plan their activities. A lot of money is spent every year in field surveys, data procurement, analysis, etc. The accuracy of data collected is not as per their expectation.

Mr. Vijayan came across satellite-based studies been used to generate crop intelligence information. He then approached two organizations and calls them for discussion. Mr. Ankur, a sales head from a Bangalore, India based company, and Mr. Dev was called. It was on two different days they were called so that the requirements can be explained, and a proposal can be obtained from them.

Day 1 meeting with Mr. Ankur and Mr. Vijayan.

Mr. Vijayan: "Hello Mr. Ankur. The reason for calling you is, we need maize crop area information for Indonesia and Bangladesh".

Mr. Ankur: "That's fine Mr. Vijayan. We can do it".

Mr. Vijayan: "Do you have experience in this?"

Mr. Ankur: "Yes we have done projects on paddy and wheat in India. We can do it for any country. We have developed the process, crop signatures, and model for crop identification using satellite images and can generate the report at any administrative unit".

Mr. Vijayan: That is nice. Can you share some notes on this?

Mr. Ankur: Sure Mr. Vijayan. We will submit the complete proposal in a couple of days.

Day 2 meeting with Mr. Dev and Mr. Vijayan

Mr. Vijayan: Hello Mr. Dev. The reason for calling you is, we need maize crop acreage information for Indonesia and Bangladesh.

Dev: "Mr. Vijayan, before we proceed, I need some more details to work on the document. If you permit, I can ask few questions on this"

Mr. Vijayan: "Please go ahead"

Dev: "As I understand you have your field team and you are in this region for some time, then what is the reason for you take up satellite-based study".

Mr. Vijayan: We have been spending a good amount of money is field surveys and data collection. The reliability and accuracy of data have been a challenge for us. We would like to test with a satellite-based study.

Dev: This is a good decision, Mr. Vijayan. Satellite-based data generation is always unbiased, and accuracy also is high. However, accuracy also depends on the spatial resolution of satellite images. I will study these two countries and get back to you in a couple of days.

Two days later, Mr. Ankur submits the full proposal with financials to Mr. Vijayan. Dev submits a concept note and visits Mr. Vijayan on the next day of note submission.

Mr. Vijayan to Dev: Dev, we have received a technical and financial proposal from one another company. But, in your document, there are no financial details.

Dev: Yes Mr. Vijayan. I need to explain some points and ask some more questions about this work. We have studies from past work that, in Bangladesh that only thirty out of sixty-four districts are major maize growing districts, hence we advise you not to go for full country mapping. This may increase the cost of the study. Similarly, in Indonesia, most of the provinces are hilly and do not grow maize. Hence about eight provinces have maize and in that also about sixty regencies out of four hundred regencies are maize growing. If we study only these regions, then it will cover the major growing areas and costs will significantly get optimized than the countrywide study.

Mr. Vijayan: This is highly informative. Yes, we need to go with that. We should not spend unnecessarily on the area where we do not have any interest.

Dev: There is one more observation Mr. Vijayan. This is regarding the sowing window in these countries. Bangladesh has dry and wet season maize. This wet season has the maximum area under maize hence we can go with one season that will cover the major portion. In Indonesia, there also wet and dry season cultivation takes place for maize. However, the planting window is slightly complicated than in other countries. This is because of the climatic pattern of that region. The planting window is about five months in the wet season and about three months in the dry season. Hence we will have to process and analyze multiple period images to arrive at the total crop acreage. Else we may miss some area.

> *"A problem well stated is a problem half solved."*
>
> – John Dewey

Mr. Vijayan: That's perfectly correct Dev. What I suggest is, we will have a common call with our Indonesia team and finalize the ideal months for which images to be taken.

Dev built confidence in Mr. Vijayan's team. The meeting followed with methodology, project schedule, and deliverable finalization. This took about two weeks. During this time Mr. Vijayan asked Mr. Ankur to revise the proposal and they changed the financials multiple times.

Once the scope, timeline, and deliverable got finalized, then Dev submitted the proposal with detailed financials. The financial negotiation took a couple of days only to finalize the payment terms and mode.

This clarifies, that identifying the problem, diagnosing the problem, and then provide the right solution will build confidence and trust among the user and the service provider.

> *"If you define the problem correctly, you almost have the solution"*
>
> **– Steve Jobs**

Skill No. 3: Be a Team Player

Eduardo Mansur, Director, Office of Climate Change, Biodiversity & Environment has mentioned in one of his speeches that, *"We cannot achieve much alone but working together we can go far, design bigger and achieve much more…"*.

Geospatial agriculture projects require multiple domains of expertise to execute and deliver the results. Consultants must demonstrate that they are team players and are willing to learn from team members, genuinely valuing the input and expertise of others. It is essential to establish a collaborative relationship with peers.

During the industrial revolution, a large number of factories or manufacturing units were set up and people joined to work in industries as skilled workers. This was the need at that time as opportunities were in industrial sectors only. These workers were assigned a specific task to do in which they were trained. They were always replaceable. To monitor their work there used to be a supervisor. The supervisor will assign the task, monitor the work, and report to management. If any worker gets ill and does not come to work, then he is replaced by another member who is trained in a similar task. This was about fifty years before and today most of our company culture has not changed. In GIS companies, we have RS/GIS designated executives, and to manage their work we have managers. Different titles are given based on their years of experience such as manager, senior manager, general manager, etc. With a sad heart, need to mention that, these managers do not play the role they are supposed to. They need to guide and mentor the young professionals and solve the problems of any executive. However, most often it is found that, if any executive has any problem, he will be treated less skilled than others and will be reported to senior management during his/her annual review. The job is the same as that of a factory supervisor. Manager's role is just to get the work done by the team by any means. Executives spend more than their actual working hours on the project. If you are a GIS executive or Manager, you will relate to this. The extra time spent by an executive is not because of the project demand but is the fear of getting replaced. This is sad to notice that it still exists in the GIS sector. This is not the fault of the system, but the individuals never molded themselves as an expert.

The need for the day is to work as a team and leave the hierarchy system. Each project should be taken as a customer problem that needs to be solved by a team of experts. The team may have experts from different fields with different years of experience. Some may have more and some fewer years of expertise. If one cannot change the system, then change oneself from being a manager to a contributor in the team to complete the task.

> THE SUCCESS OF TEAMWORK: *"Coming together is beginning, keeping together is progress, working together is success"*
>
> **– Henry Ford**

A team player is someone who actively contributes to their group to manage projects. Team players actively listen to their coworkers, respect feedbacks, and aim to enhance the project quality. Team players understand that their team's success is their success, and they share responsibilities.

The contribution by a team player should not be by any compulsion or force but it is his willingness to help team members and learn from others. S/he should have the commitment and responsibilities towards the success of a project.

> *"The strength of the team is each individual member. The strength of each member is the team."*
>
> – Phil Jackson

Skill No. 4: Discipline

Discipline as we all know is the key to success. Without discipline, there is no life at all. If one has a passion to work on geospatial agriculture, then your passion can get you started but it is the discipline that will keep you moving. With discipline, one can achieve good to great results. Great consultants work hard, they work smart and they work with discipline. They know how to accomplish the best results in the shortest possible time with as little friction as possible. Great consultants are problem solvers: bring them in and the work gets done.

In the context of the application of geospatial technology in agriculture, it is the art and creativity that an individual must bring in to get the best of the results. The definition of agriculture says it is the science and art of cultivating plants and livestock. Similarly, image interpretation, boundary delineation, is an art. Working with a satellite image is like making art. An artist requires canvas, paint, brush, creative ideas, the combination of colors, and discipline to make the best art. Similarly, crop mapping or land use land cover mapping or soil mapping using remote sensing and GIS is like an art that needs, satellite image, interpretation keys to think on tone, texture, pattern, association, discipline to work on every known pixel, discipline while delineating boundaries, can bring the best-classified maps for the users.

Another important part of discipline is attitude. Attitude can be read through expressions, voice, and inflections. When our attitude is right, our abilities reach a maximum of effectiveness and great results inevitably follow. Attitudes do make a difference. It makes you effective in dealing with people, enable you to develop as a leader.

Time is also a crucial part of the discipline. Time refers to the management of project deadlines, shipment dates. A consultant must submit the results as per the project's deadlines. Since the consultant would have done all the planning and estimates before taking the project in hand hence, s/he must stick to the timeline. This is one side to show sincerity. There will always be a scope to improve the quality of results if given more time. Some of the agriculture projects are extremely critical. If we miss the time, then a stage of the crop can be lost. Similarly, if there is a delay in the submission of results for trading or insurance organizations then the critical part of decision making based on crop condition at that time is lost. Hence managing time is very essential.

Giving value to time is one of the finest qualities one should have in consulting. As we know that consulting is more of a relationship building. Hence giving value to time plays an especially important role in consulting. If you are called for a meeting or if you have called a meeting then, you should be on time. You should not delay in reaching the meeting. The time of every individual who is participating in a meeting should be given respect.

Dev's always quotes his father's statement to his students, "For any meeting, you should reach before time. You can wait for other members but never allow other members to wait for you. Despite their position, whether senior or junior. If you give value to other's time, then in the future your time will be valued. This can build a strong relationship".

To become a successful trusted consultant, one needs nothing more than few simple disciplines, practiced every task at hand.

Skill No. 5: Hunger to learn

Great consultants never stop learning. They need to stay on top of the happenings in their fields of capability. It is their job to bring the latest knowledge and skills to the table when others cannot. An individual who does not thrive by constantly learning additional components of their industry will become stale and will soon find their opportunities declining.

> *Education is the most powerful weapon which you can use to change the world*
>
> **– Nelson Mandela**

Dev, our geospatial agriculture consultant, when he was young and has joined a multinational company for the first time after having worked with a research and development organization, was given a role to lead a project team. He was then having three to four years of working experience. It was an agriculture crop information creation for six states of India. Dev was good at the soil, land use land cover mapping, and watershed management projects based on his experience. He knew the concepts of crop mapping but has not handled any commercial project by then. His role was only to manage the team, get the work done on time, and prepare project reports based on the results submitted by the team. (Dev was good at documentation as he had experience of working in technical documentation, proposal preparation, and presentation preparation in his earlier organization).

Dev took this project as an opportunity to learn a new technique. Rather than focusing on people management and report writing work, he spent time with the team supporting them in their work and indirectly learning the techniques. Dev used to work with the team and spend extra hours learning. The team was fortunate as a senior member was working with them, giving confidence to the team and the team also got extra support in execution.

This is how Dev keeps learning whenever he gets an opportunity. Dev always gives example to his students and colleagues from one of the Indian movie "Three Idiots" where the lead actor tells his friends that "obtaining an education is not only by following a system and sitting in classrooms, but you should obtain it from any place where knowledge is being shared".

Dev became technically very capable and he used to take up certification courses every year from different organizations such as FAO, UNCCLERN, Coursera, Future learn, AgMOOCS, etc. At the age of 39 and after a gap of 12 years from his formal education Dev took up a Master's in Business Administration. At the age of 42, he took up a certification course and became a certified advisor.

Recently when I met Dev and I found him studying and learning from a young guy. I was curious to find out that at the age when he is nearing 50, and when he teaches hundreds of students is learning like a student. I went to his residence and asked him about this.

Me: "Hi Dev! How are you? And How is everything going on at your end?

Dev: "I am fine, doing good. Thanks for asking"

Me: "It seems you are busy studying and doing some work on your laptop. Is it the right time to talk or shall I come later?"

Dev: "It is fine, I am doing my homework given by my friend's subordinate who is teaching me"

Me: "I am surprised to know that you are learning at this age. Is it required for you? You have a team, and you can recommend hiring anyone to get the job done"

Dev: "Yes this is the reason why I am learning. I know about optical remote sensing and have been doing a lot of projects using that. Recently there were requirements to work during the wet season in the Southeast Asia region where most of the time it will be clouded. To work in such conditions, we have planned to work using microwave data. Hence we are going to hire a couple of experts in microwave remote sensing".

Me: "Then, if you are hiring, your job is done. They can handle the project"

Dev: "I should know the subject to assess the candidates. I should also know the subject if I have to give them any task. I should be aware of the task any of my team members is doing. I should be able to help them if they get stuck at any place with basic concepts. Besides, I will be able to support the team in case of the absence of any member for any reason. Another most important reason is, I should be able to answer my client about the process we have adopted in achieving the result".

Me: "This is inspiring, Dev"

Dev: "I believe that there is no age or position for learning. Keep learning. Growth and success depend on your learning. It is not always that you should learn from school or courses, you can learn by reading books, watching videos, or by listening to podcasts"

The illiterate of the future will not be the person who cannot read. It will be the person who does not know how to learn.

– **Alvin Toffler**

Now we are clear that "Why do any organization hire a consultant". This is because a consultant can solve the problem. Consultants are hired for the work that client or his team cannot do. This is the reason that consultants should keep learning and always be updated on their subjects.

"Always be smarter than the people who hire you."

– **Lena Horne**

Skill No.6: Good Listening Skills

During the consulting process, consultants will meet different people with unique characteristics. Some will be verbose, others reticent. Having excellent listening skills will encourage all to talk freely. This leads to more information sharing which, in the end, can make the consulting process more streamlined.

Good listening has two benefits. The first: it allows the listener to understand clearly what the other person is trying to communicate. The second: gives importance to the words of the speaker which makes him share more of his problem or ideas. The other party feels; heard and understood.

Skill No. 7: Good Communication skills

Excellent oral and written communication skills are a must for a consultant. Since consultants are often viewed as the subject matter expert (SME), s/he should be able to effectively communicate the ideas. Some of the key communication areas for a consultant are delivering clear training sessions, providing accurate documentation, asking the right questions, writing emails with clarity, etc.

In the geospatial sector, the roles are defined based on communication skills and technical capability. For an individual to grow, he must work on his technical as well as communication skills. Let us understand this with the four-quadrant diagram given below. In one of the axes, we have communication skills from low to high, and in another axis, we have technical capability from low to high.

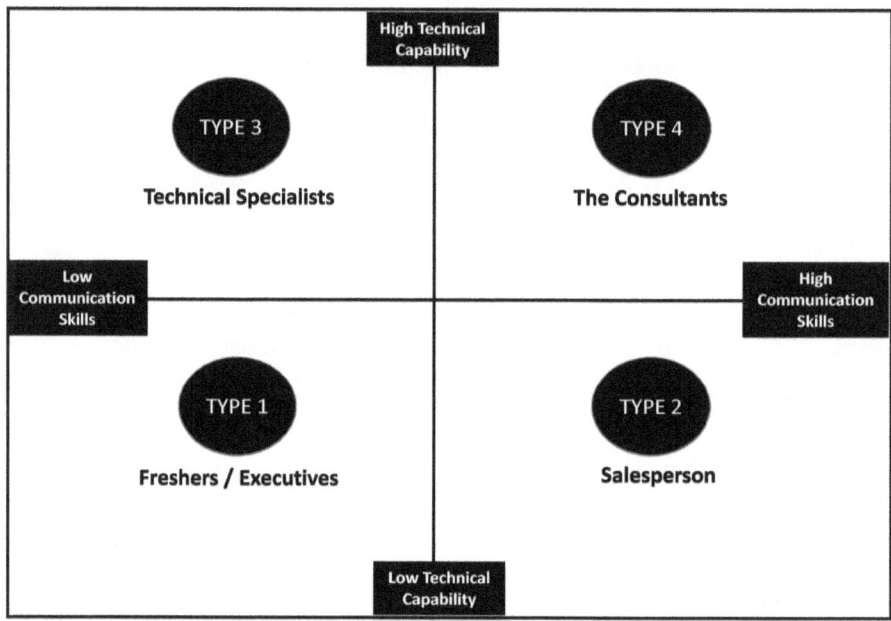

Type 1: Low communication skills and low technical capability – These are mostly the freshers, interns, and newly joined executives. They learn technical skills and communication skills to get promoted to the higher ladder with new roles and responsibilities. However, in the geospatial sector, it is found that some individuals do not improve their communication skills and do not learn any new technology, which remains at the executive level. Some executives keep learning new techniques and become an expert in their area of work. Some improve their communication skills and technical

competency to become experts in their domain. Few executives get attracted by people with high communication skills. These are individuals who are in sales. They travel a lot, attend conferences, do client calls, and are close to management. Looking at these some freshers choose this path to get into type 2 class.

Type 2: High Communication skills and low technical capabilities - These are mostly the salespeople in the geospatial sector. Some are smart to win projects with their effective communication skills. Whereas, at times with low technical capability these types of individuals overcommit and underdeliver the projects. They always need the support of Type 3 categories of people to work in their sales leads.

Type 3: Low Communication skills and High Technical Capability – These are the experts and are the individuals who are working on projects, leading teams, and do the shipments to clients. They are poor in articulating their work and communicating it with ease to clients. The technical experts must pass through Type 2 and learn a few smart communication skills to become type 4 which is consultants. This category of people very certainly can become consultants (Type4).

Type 4: High communication skills and high technical capability – These are the Consultants, who are responsible for the growth of the team and organization. They work on the project from its development till its submission. With their right communication skills, they can understand the client's needs, define the problem of the client, design the scope of work and deliver the project as per the requirement of the client. They continue with their communication skills to follow-up with clients for long-term relationships.

Skill No. 8: Flexible

Adaptability is one of the essential skills that a good consultant needs to have. The projects will change, the team may change, the place may differ, and the work culture may differ. Hence good consultants adapt to changes easily. They come in, they fit in and they get the job done. Their soft skills and technical expertise allow them to take on their roles quickly and easily. Flexibility offers tremendous productivity improvement. Flexibility also allows more creativity and innovation in the table.

Adapting to work from anywhere also is part of workplace flexibility. This allows a consultant to focus their energy on work and life. As an individual, you must give more attention to the importance of work-life balance, to be in a better position to decide and act more holistically on what is important and urgent to them.

Skill No. 9: Professionalism

Professionalism implies that you do not focus only on the immediate transaction, but care about your relationship with the person with whom you are working. Professionalism is an amalgamation of knowledge, skills, technical competence, attitude, discipline, being ethical, and self-control. Consultants should always keep in mind that client relationships should remain at a professional level. Building professional relationships is critical for project success, and when done effectively, consultants can swiftly become a client's trusted advisor.

We all know one does not get a second chance to make a first impression. Everything from how you greet others, how you dress, the words you choose, your tone of voice, your table manners, the respect you extend to others... everything favors your professional rating.

A client will value consultant if both continue to work together in a collaborative process, well understood, communicated to all, and focused on results. As a consultant communicate clearly what you are going to do and do what you have communicated. By this, you can be clear and consistent with the work. At times there will be different opinions from the client's side if they have a big team working on the project. At that time, as a consultant, one has to listen patiently and encourage a diverse perspective and then come out with a solution beneficial for the project.

In consulting projects, it is always better to go slow with the client rather than going faster without the client. Besides, there is no blame is consulting relations.

The client perceives you to be authentic and respectful, and to do the task with a focus on results and learning. Similarly, as a consultant, you should also expect the same level of professionalism from the client. It has been observed that, as a GIS service provider in the Agriculture sector, you are mostly considered as a vendor. Most of the large agriculture multinationals first do the vendor registration of the consulting firms before signing a project. The GIS or consulting firm will be treated equally as any other seller, retailer, or supplier. The consultant must go through the administration and accounts department. Hence as a consultant, you have all the benefits to choose your customer similarly to the client has.

"Professionalism: It's not the job you do, it's how you do the job."

Consulting Competency Framework

Dev helped us understand, how these technical and soft skills are important for an individual to become a trusted consultant. The consulting skills from technical to behavior skills can be combinedly put into a framework which is *"Geospatial Agriculture Consulting Competency Framework"*. This framework has five broad categories such as technical competency, business competency, consulting competency, consulting skills, and behavior. Any project or work worth doing involves some of the basic qualities other than the key qualities mentioned above. These qualities should be part of everyone's life whether you are a consultant or not.

The first one is **Hard Work**. Recently a lot has been spoken about smart work rather than hard work. The difference between hard work and smart work is based on how you approach any task. Hard work would mean spending long hours to complete work without any shortcuts. Smart work would be aiming for the same results but with planning and prioritization of tasks. The smart work has been misinterpreted by some and has been done with shortcuts and manipulations. The term often used for this in the geospatial sector is "Jugaad" in place of smart work. English dictionary Oxford has officially accepted the word 'Jugaad' in its latest update. According to the dictionary, the noun Jugaad means a flexible approach to solve a problem, that innovatively uses limited resources.

The second one is **Positivity**. Here is a consultant positivity refers to creating a positive work environment, motivating team, exchange of feedbacks with positive intentions, no blame game, mentoring, and coaching. You will observe in companies that, if bad feedback is received from a client on a project, it is immediately put on to the team working on it. And at times, CEOs will fire the team members rather than finding the fault and solving it. Dev mentioned that in this career he has received much feedback from the client. But he has never passed that to the team working him. He takes that as a lesson to correct the approach and not to repeat the same mistake in the next project.

The third quality is **Integrity**. Honesty and truthfulness in any task should be the prime quality of an individual and for the company. Some of the examples of integrity are being open and honest when communicating with others. Holding yourself accountable and owning up to your shortcomings when leading a team.

The fourth quality that a consultant must have is **Confidence.** Good consultants are confident about their skills and expertise. They leave their egos at the door. This makes them team players and they put company goals and team spirit first.

> *"Confidence comes from years of constant work, dedication, discipline, and training."*

The fifth quality is the **Ability to work under pressure.** Agriculture is often a high-stress profession, whether it is driven by extensive climatic conditions, having a tough client, or tight project timelines. Tight project timelines are because of the crop duration. If the results are delayed, then any critical stage for decision making will be missed. Mostly, the team helping you meet those deadlines are not within your control. It is a consultant's or leader's job to remain steady and continue to motivate the team to meet their obligations.

> *To be successful you have to deal with CRAP. Criticism, Rejection, Assholes, and Pressure.*
>
> **– Ryan Blair**

At times there will be false pressure created. This usually happens when the management is unaware of the subject. And they do not value the skills of experts. Dev once shared an incident about a project he was executed for a customer. He submitted his proposal with a project schedule that detailed about 16 weeks to complete the project. The project was for a client who has invested in a large piece of land in Africa. The scope of work included land evaluation, crop suitability zonation, and agriculture land use planning using remote sensing and GIS technique. The work included satellite image selection and processing, pre-field mapping, reconnaissance survey, and soil sample collection, soil sample analysis, post field map finalization analysis of thematic layers, and finally planning with the recommendation by taking the help of other subject matter experts.

Dev presented the approach and schedule to the client. To this the CEO of that company mentioned, "If I provide you additional five resources can you complete the work in 8 weeks. This way we will save time and get more profit". Dev responded and explained that each step is linked with the other. Unless the first step is done one cannot move to the next step. And software takes its own time for processing and analysis. This is where the knowledge, expertise, and communication skills play an important role for a consultant.

> "No matter how great the talent or efforts, some things just take time. You can't produce a baby in one month by getting nine women pregnant."
>
> – Warren Buffett

GEOSPATIAL AGRICULTURE CONSULTING COMPETENCY FRAMEWORK

Technical Competency	Agriculture Subject Knowledge		Geospatial Technology Expertise		
Business Competency	Agribusiness understanding (Key Stakeholders in Agriculture viz. input industry, farming community, commodity trading groups, agriculture insurance providers, government departments, researchers, students etc.)				
Consulting Competency	Trust Building	User Need Assessment	Client Engagement (Developing solution, delivering the solution / service and continuing future relation)		
Consulting Skills	Problem Solver	Team Player	Hunger to Learn	Work under Pressure	Adaptability
	Hard Work	Confidence	Listening and Communication		
Basic Behavior	Positivity		Integrity		Professionalism

Recapitulate

Dear readers. In the previous two sections, we have understood about realizing self-potential based on the knowledge, expertise, and experience one must make personal readiness towards consulting. It is also an understanding of self-competencies and capabilities towards solving a customer problem.

The second chapter explained a mindset shift. In this, we discussed how an agriculture expert or a geospatial expert can shift his or her thinking from just being a "doer" to a "Problem Solver". The purpose of this book is to develop as many geospatial agriculture experts as possible so that agriculture problems of key stakeholders can be solved and improvement in agriculture can be achieved. Wayne Dyer quoted: "When you change the way you look at things, the things you look at change."

In the following chapter, we discussed the key myths that block an individual to perform to its potential. These are also called "Self-limiting beliefs". These myths were explained, and the truth was presented in the chapter to make a clear path for an individual to get into geospatial agriculture consulting.

The fourth chapter was the key chapter because the knowledge you have and the experience of working in your niche area you carry is not sufficient to become a consultant. There is a need for some key qualities to present yourself to the customer, and project team towards meeting the goal of the project or company.

Whatever we learned till this stage is all about our knowledge and qualities that we must either develop or polish. These are internal qualities and skills. These are consulting competencies that an individual must work on himself.

The next three sections will describe the external environment of consulting. These are the consulting approach to face clients, win projects, and solve customer problems. Followed by this, we will discuss the type of consulting role you can choose based on your limitation or convenience.

In the end, we will find out some risks and reasons for failures in consulting business. Most of the time we learn the positive side and take the step. This site teaches, what to do, how to do etc. But we should always be aware of the side that teaches, what not to do. This chapter will list nine key reasons taken from the other consulting business failures, that will help us learn from their mistakes and we will be more careful. Mistakes have the power to turn you into something better than you were before.

Julie Dirksen quoted: "Learning experiences are like journeys. The journey starts where the learning is now and ends when the learner is successful. The end of the journey isn't knowing more, it's doing more"

Section 3

Learn

Recognize Uncover **Learn** Engage Secure

Chapter 5

Consulting Framework

As a consultant, you work with clients to solve problems. To solve any problem, you need to follow the approach of consulting. This consulting approach can be broadly be arranged into five stages. This includes defining the problem, assessing/diagnosing the problem, analyzing the key elements of problems, implementation/ execution, results/shipment with recommendations, and finally, evaluating the results towards extension, replication, or termination.

Nine-step geospatial agriculture consulting framework to problem-solving

The consulting framework is the system, process, and overall approach a consultant uses to develop the solutions to the client's problems. Consulting methodologies are a professionally designed framework of information and analyses. The analyses a consultant develops should be based on a proven and structured system of geospatial technology and tools to resolve the client's issues beneficially. This framework is designed as a set of tasks to be completed in a logical order.

A nine-step framework to problem-solving

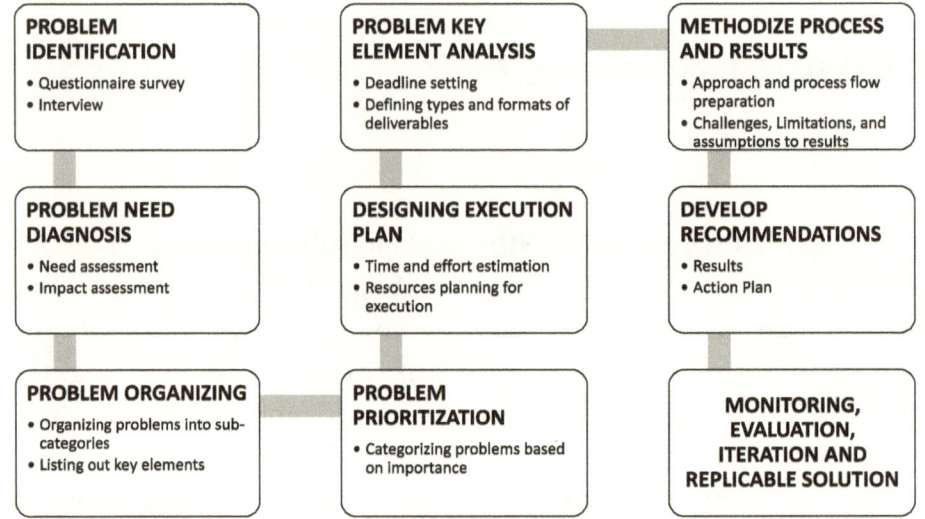

Step 1: Identify and define the problem

This is the first and important stage of problem-solving. In this step, the problem is identified by a consultant through a questionnaire-based survey or interview. The consultant asks questions to the client to arrive at the problem definition. This is usually a two-way approach where it is not only the consultant asking the question, whereas the consultant discussing similar problems and solutions through his experience. This ensures that consultants and clients are on the same page and answering the same question. For a consultant, this stage is to identify the exact problem that the client is having. And for a client, this stage is to assess the consultant's competency and capabilities.

Let us understand this through one of Dev's experience of dealing with a client.

Mr. Rohan is the program coordinator for a project on the Agriculture livelihood development program in one of the tehsils (sub-district) of the state in southern India. This district falls in hot and dry climatic regions. The program is under implementation for the past three years. The results on agriculture for increasing farmer's crop yield were not satisfactory. However, the other areas of education, health and sanitation areas were performing well under the program.

Mr. Rohan is young and believes in digital technology. He was told by someone about satellite image-based crop information generation. He got in contact with Dev and the discussion began between them.

Rohan: "Hello Dev. We need a scientific approach that can provide Pigeon Pea and Groundnut crop information on its acreage, health, and production for the project study area which is the tehsil. The second requirement is to develop a crop management practices manual. Will you or your company be able to provide us agriculture information using satellite images?".

Dev: "Hello Rohan. I will be able to help you out with this. But before that, I need to understand the project in detail. Hope it is fine with you to share. Can you please share those?"

Rohan: "Sure. I will do that."

Dev: "What is the project all about and why do you need crop-related information?"

Rohan: "We are a not-for-profit organization, and we are working on an agriculture livelihood development program. In this Agriculture, our main objective is to increase the crop yield per acre. We have implemented the project for the past two years which is four seasons (two Kharif and two rabis). This is a five-year project. We have followed the standard crop management practices and have supplied the high yielding varieties (obtained from the agriculture research center) to selected farmers under the demonstration. The same variety is performing differently from different farmers' fields. We have done tank development by desilting. With two monsoons, the water level in the tanks has increased. But surprisingly the yields have not improved as they were expected. Hence we need to understand the overall *crop status of the tehsil before the implementation of the program and then for the current year so that a comparative analysis can be performed".*

Dev was listening carefully and was making a note. After Rohan completed, Dev gave a pause for a minute and shared his viewpoints.

Dev: "As I understand, the overall objective of the project is to improve the livelihood of farmers growing pigeon pea and groundnut. For this, you have planned for improvement through an increase in yield by which income of farmer will increase which will ultimately improve his livelihood".

Rohan: Yes, that is what we need. Will you or your organization be able to do this for us?"

Dev: "Yes we can. But I feel there is something more required in the project. We have done similar studies for Sugarcane and Paddy using satellite images. We have also done similar projects in Africa".

Rohan: "This is wonderful. You have the expertise and experience. I think we should go ahead discussing further on this project. Can you please submit the proposal with financials? This will help us in working out the project funds."

Step 2: Diagnose the problem or project need assessment

The second step in consulting is to need assessment of the project to arrive at the proposed results. For this, the consultant and the client must arrive at the exact pain point. This step also deals with the impact it will create for the end-users.

After going through the work progress report, Dev meets Rohan after a couple of days to present his assessment report.

Dev presents his brief user needs assessment note. He mentions that, based on the research done on the project area landscape, climatic patterns, agriculture practices, and available source of irrigation, he found that the project area has different physiography. The lands are plain near the river while it is undulating in uplands. The soils are deep in the plains to shallow and gravelly in uplands. Soils are also found to be of fine texture (clayey and loamy) at someplace and coarse-textured (sandy) at some places. The project area has water bodies, but most of them are shallow and dry. The source of irrigation for the majority of agriculture cultivated areas is rainfall and a small portion of lands are irrigated through tank water.

Hence the key problems that need to be solved would be improving the agricultural land resources such as soil quality, availability of water resources for irrigation, providing farmer's the good and certified high yielding varieties of seeds, training farmers on sustainable agriculture practices, and monitoring of the program as per the designed action plan. Dev concludes his presentation by giving his broad project scope of work.

"This looks good and in the broader picture, it is covering all the areas such as land, water, farmers, and management practices", Rohan remarks after listening to the Dev's presentation.

"Dev, I request if you can work out the details of the project in similar lines that you have presented then we can take it forward. Meanwhile, we can finalize your consulting agreement as a consultant for this project. Later based on detailed analysis, we can work on the team required or firm to be hired, etc." Rohan submits his concluding remark for that day.

Step 3: Organize the Problem

A well-organized problem always results in good smooth execution of the project. To effectively execute the problem, one needs to organize the key elements or resources. One of the most important reasons for keeping a to-do list is the organization. Organizing your tasks with a list can make everything much more manageable and make you feel grounded. Seeing a clear outline of your completed and uncompleted tasks will help you feel organized and stay focused.

Dev works on the details of the project sub-activities. He submits the project organizing plan, where he mentions the phases of studies that will cover the broad objectives and meet the project requirements. He advised that the project will be divided into phase wise execution.

The first phase of the project will be on natural resources inventory creation. This will include mapping of land use land cover, soil (including soil survey, soil sampling, and soil analysis), slope (using Digital elevation model), physiography (landforms), drainage patterns (streams and water bodies).

Part "b" of phase one will be the farmer's interview to be conducted by subject matter experts to understand the crop management practices they are following. Also to get information about agriculture income, other sources of income, expenses. This will give us a basic knowledge of the areas of improvement required.

The second phase will include the analysis of these maps to carry out Land evaluation and crop suitability zonation. Another analysis will be carried out to identify suitable sites for water harvesting structures, deepening of only selected tanks that are essential for irrigation, and improvement of stream course for the free flow of rainwater.

The third phase of the project will include site-specific crop management practices manual preparation. This will be based on the land characteristics and limitations. Recommendations will be provided based on the land evaluation and crop suitability classes.

The fourth phase will be to identify farmers from each suitability zones where the demonstration will be performed. These farmers will be provided training by the project team of experts on the land resources development activities. Improved varieties will be provided to these groups of farmers.

The second part of the fourth phase will be on water resources development. A second team will be formed which will work in close coordination with the local development organization. The water resources plan map will be sued to implement the developmental activities.

Rohan: This sounds perfect and scientific. This way will have the complete picture of the tehsil (sub-district). The demonstration farms can be monitored and evaluated carefully. Based on success stories, these can be replicated to larger areas.

Rohan continues and suggests that to optimize the project cost, he will provide all the human resource support for the field survey, training, and implementation work. He asks Dev to look for the subject matter experts who can lead their respective areas of work such as Agriculture, water, documentation, etc.

Followed by assessment, the client team finalizes the scope of work, project schedule, team, etc., and then the financials are discussed with the Dev's consulting team, and the project is taken for execution.

As in the example we have observed, for each phase of the project, the problem, its activities, and deliverables need to be organized. This will require organizing your resources well in advances such as human resources (the team, including the support staff), financial resources (the money - get advance payment from the client to mobilize resources), project inputs (any input that is relevant for the project must be organized before the start of the project) and infrastructure such as hardware, software, etc related to project activities. Consider all the factors that could be influencing the situation and then structure the problem into categories.

If your project activities are not meticulously organized, tasks can pile up, work gets lost, and valuable time is spent on finding information that should be readily available. However, good organizational skills can make or break a project, ultimately saving you time and reducing stress.

Step 4: Prioritize Issues

On any given day, prioritizing not only makes a person more efficient at daily work-related activities but also gives them the latitude to focus on their personal goals. It helps strike the right balance to handle both, their professional and personal life. Likewise, in any project execution, Prioritizing increases the success rates of strategic projects, increase the alignment, and focus of team members around project goals, clears all doubts for the operational actions when faced with decisions, and, most important, builds an execution outlook and culture

Project prioritization gives you and your team an easy-to-follow plan for the work that needs to be done, while also setting clear expectations for your client or organization. In other words, it sets everyone up for success.

A simple prioritization technique can be followed. Identify the issues that are the most important. This saves time by not considering aspects that are not relevant. The most used Urgent-Important technique can also be followed. This has four categories

- Urgent and Important: Make these your top priority.
- Urgent and Not Important: Put them second on your list.
- Not Urgent and Important: While these may not be time-pressing, they still need to get done.
- Not urgent and not important: These can be avoided if it can or can be taken up when all other tasks are completed.

Priorities will guide the team and keep the project on track. Most importantly, priorities will give you the confidence to say "no" to the least important tasks.

The purpose of prioritization is to allocate resources to the most important work first followed by the least priority tasks.

Prioritization provides a focus—WHERE to assign resources and WHEN to start the work. The goal of prioritization is to accomplish the most important work to deliver maximum business value.

Step 5: Design Execution Plan

Project Execution Plan – This is related to the way the problem is structured. The way the problem is broken up will become the work modules. An execution plan consists of three components: milestones, tasks, and budgets. Milestones are your key project goals. Tasks are the specific things you need to do to reach each milestone. The third component, your budget, details how much your plan will cost.

Design Execution Plans will be required to ensure that the results/ solution will be delivered to an agreed method and approach. The Project Execution Plan is the central document that determines the means to execute, monitor, and control project activities. The plan serves as the main communication vehicle to ensure that everyone is aware and knowledgeable of project objectives and how they will be accomplished. It is a document describing how, when and by whom a specific target or set of targets is to be achieved. These targets will include the project's products, timescales, costs, quality, and benefits.

Step 6: Conduct Project Key Element Analysis

Essential elements must be included to create a good project plan. These key elements need to be analyzed critically for better execution. Broadly for any project, the key elements that need to be analyzed are:

- Client requirement analysis
- Process Analysis

- Staffs/Team member analysis
- Financial analysis
- Risk/Threat analysis

Timeline, costs, and deliverables should be detailed clearly to show the scope of your project.

Clients need framework: Before starting your project, it is essential to align the team with the project's goals and needs. The team also needs to be summarized on the importance of any specific project to the organizational objectives. And finally, the team should have clarified stakeholder's expectations.

List of requirements and project objectives: As an expert, you should analyze the needs of all groups involved in the project and define the requirements to achieve them. The features, formats, and type of deliverables should be clearly defined. Even though a project plan is a designed document, but it is sure to change during the project, or as the project progresses, there may be a need to correct some aspects of your project plan and that is okay.

Resource allocation

When it comes to resource allocation in project planning, the first is to choose the competent resource for the project and then you break down and allocate your team's time, materials, and budget. In the geospatial sector, it is quite common that any person who knows a bit of GIS and remote sensing works in any kind of project. The resource at times also works in multiple projects. Be it an urban project or be it an agriculture project. They are not the best resource for the project, but they are just to fit in. Later they spend time and money in training these resources before getting into execution. And at times they are not even trained. In that situation, the resources must take the help of the internet and complete the project. This way the results are not as per the expectation of the client. The quality is reduced. Being a geospatial agriculture expert, you are the best resource for agriculture-based projects.

During resource analysis, you need to consider resource constraints, how much time each resource can realistically devote to this project, and determine the best combinations or variations of the resources available to achieve the project's goals in the allotted time, and with the best possible results.

Defined roles and responsibilities

One of the most important of key elements analysis is to bring clarity on the roles of the responsibilities of team members. Clarify the responsibilities of each person on the project team, including the external stakeholders such as surveys or other vendors. The client funds the project, and they may need to review and approve critical aspects of the plan. Designated geospatial agriculture experts along with business experts define requirements for projects and deliverables. The consultant along with other experts creates, executes, and controls the project plan. And the project team completes the tasks and builds the end-product.

For any project defining the roles of the support team such as finance, administration, procurement, etc., is equally important. Any delay from their end can interrupt the project completely.

Project deliverables list and project timeline

From the preparation of the project scope statement, you should now have a clearer idea of the deliverables and outcomes to be delivered to complete this project. From there, you should list out what tasks and deliverables each team member is expected to produce and when.

A work breakdown structure is typically the best way to achieve this step. You can use a simple list, flow chart, spreadsheet, or Gantt chart to map out all the project work, assign to teammates, set due dates, and mark any dependencies.

In this breakdown, it is also necessary to note which deliverables or tasks will need to be approved by external stakeholders and ensure there are no delays due to task dependencies or reviews and approvals.

A detailed project schedule should guide in the timelines to be achieved. The project schedule is simply one of many components of a project plan. In a project schedule, you estimate how long it will take to complete each task while leaving enough room for slack and dependencies. It is a clear calendarization of all required tasks and timelines. It shows the project's duration, who is doing what, and when each task begins and ends.

Risk assessment plan

It is crucial to assess the risks involved with a project while creating the project plan. As an expert, you should be aware of potential risks, hazards, and opportunities that could come from executing this project. At the same time, you should be ready with your mitigation plan.

Potential risk events identified in your project plan may not happen, but they could significantly affect a project's outcome if they did. Risk assessment and management includes not just assessing the risk itself but developing risk management plans to communicate how the team should respond if these events happen.

If you can identify risks earlier in a project, you can control them and increase your chances of success.

Quality checking (QC) and Quality assurance (QA)

Quality analysis is a set of steps to examine and investigate a certain project activity and identify what enhances the activity's value.

The goal of project quality analysis is to review quality levels and define necessary improvements in the existing quality management framework. The best skills of an expert are to maintain project quality throughout the project's execution that the final deliverable meets the customer specifications. The emphasis here is on preventing errors, rather than inspecting the final deliverable at the end of the project. Creating the QA plan involves setting the project standards, acceptance criteria, and metrics that will be used throughout the project. This becomes the foundation for all quality reviews and inspections performed during the project.

In a typical GIS project, the QA/QC will happen near the end. The closer we reach to project shipment, there will be more meetings, more people involved, and more likely the CEO's involvement. This is only to show the position presence. Sometimes it works and most of the time the work is redone to add the points suggested by the CEO. The closer the project gets to completion; the fewer people should see it and fewer changes should be permissible.

Step 7: Methodology and approach preparation

A methodology gives the path. The term is also used as an approach or process flow for the project. Preparing a suitable and sound approach that is right for your project will give you the path to success. A methodology will give you the guidelines to make your project manageable, and effective. The general aim of the project methodology is to be able to standardize, structure, and organize work methods. The methodology can be defined as

"Project Management Methodology is a strictly defined combination of logically related practices, methods, and processes that determine how best to plan, develop, control, and deliver a project throughout the continuous implementation process until successful completion and termination. It is a scientifically-proven, systematic and disciplined approach to project design, execution, and completion."

Typically, a methodology provides a skeleton for describing every step in detail, so that the project lead (consultant) will know what to do to deliver and implement the work according to the schedule, budget, and client specification.

The purpose of the project methodology is to control the entire process through the effective decision making and problem-solving while ensuring the success of specific processes, techniques, and technologies.

Step 8: Synthesize results with recommendations

Result synthesis at times referred to as literature review is to answer the client question on, "What do all the findings mean for the client?". A good consultant can synthesize all the evidence and tell the client very clearly what was found and what they should do.

Your collected data must be combined into a coherent whole and accompanied by an analysis that conveys a deeper understanding of the body of evidence. The purpose is to conclude the findings so that you can identify how the literature addresses your research question.

The process includes Gathering literature that addresses the client's problem statement; Review literature to describe, summarize, analyze, and identify key concepts and Synthesize literature to compare, evaluate, interpret so that you can conclude.

Step 9: Evaluate the findings

Project evaluation is a valuable tool for consultants who are seeking to strengthen the quality of their projects and improve outcomes for the customers they serve. Evaluation is also essential to ensure that limited resources are utilized most efficiently for the greatest possible impact. As a process, project evaluation takes a series of steps to identify and measure the outcomes and impacts resulted from project completion.

Some of the common methods at can be used to evaluate GIS-based projects are customer feedbacks, Implementation reviews, Questionnaires, Interviews.

Some of the benefits of evaluation include:

- Enhancing the probability that the project objectives are being achieved
- Determining value for money (i.e., allocated resources are yielding the greatest benefit for clients and stakeholders)
- Identifying what components of an initiative work/do not work and why
- Identifying areas that need improvement to provide the best service possible

To summarize, the 9 key steps in consulting framework are

- Identify the problem
- Diagnose the pain points
- Organize the problem(s)
- Prioritize the ley activities of problem
- Design execution plan
- Analyze the key elements of the project
- Prepare methodology or approach
- Generate results or recommendations
- Evaluate results for scaling or closure

Dev said to Sunil, "There is no one best framework and often you may find that you are using multiple frameworks in the implementation process to solve your client problem. Frameworks save you time by providing a starting point for understanding the pain points through information gathering and analysis. But we must remember: the most powerful framework you have is your expertise and common sense. These tools are time-savers, but ultimately it is your insight that will deliver value to your client. As a consultant, clients hire you to solve a problem or pain point. Frameworks are useful tools that help you analyze the issue, structure your thinking, and provide solutions".

"As a consultant, I understand the problem, study the value of data and use my ability to shape that information into a satisfying solution"

Chapter 6

Approach to Consultative Selling

"Don't find customers for your products, find products for your customers"

– Seth Godin

Consultative selling is a sales approach that prioritizes relationships and open dialogue to identify and provide solutions to a customer's needs. It is focused on the customer, rather than the product being sold.

The approach of Consultative selling is a needs-based selling approach that focuses on building a relationship with a customer or prospect, understanding their problems, and developing solutions to their challenges through open-ended questions and active listening.

For a consultant to get into consultative selling, it is all about three main things, mindset, skills, and practice. One must shift his mindset from transaction selling to consultative selling.

There can be two situations where one can apply consultative selling. One when a customer approaches you (the consultant), to find a solution for his problem. The second is when you (the consultant) do the selling by finding a customer.

The first type of customer does market research, studies skills, and capabilities of consultant(s), and then approaches a few of them who can help him out in reaching his desired goal. The customer knows the goal where he needs to reach. He evaluates the best expert who can take him to his desired stage. He may or may not know his problem or limitations that are stopping him to reach the goal. In such a case, the consultant identifies the problem, diagnoses the problem, works on the problem, and provides the solution to reach the desired goal.

The five-step process of consultative selling when a customer finds a consultant is

The second situation is where the consultant does his market research. He knows his target market and target customer segment. He uses his skills, proven case studies, and solutions or products (websites, blogs, papers, books, etc.) to create interest among the customers. He builds the relation to identifying the potential customer must reach a better goal that the customer has not thought of. He shows the path by which both can go together to achieve better results than the current situation.

The five-step process of consultative selling when consultant looks for a prospect is

Let us understand these one-by-one

1. Explore

Before initiating contact with potential customers, it's wise to devote ample time to research them and their business. Part of that research is lead qualification. The customer can be called a qualified lead, if he is the person making the decision, if he is the authority to take a call on budget, and most important is if the person has in-depth knowledge about the requirement and pain points. Simultaneously, explore your competitive service providers. Analyze your strength that another consultant or the firm does not have. Proper research means becoming an expert in the buyer's business and to be ready with questions to ask for getting an answer that can make your consulting solution simpler.

2. Ask

The customer may have one or many problems. The customer may be or may not be aware of the cause of the problem. For a consultant to understand how a problem can be identified and diagnosed, you need to ask the right questions.

Asking may sound simple, but the simplest things are often the hardest to get right. To build a relationship, ask simple, basic, and open-ended questions and let the client do the talking. The open-ended questions can give an elaborative answer, rather than questions that can be answered "yes" or "no".

Through many research studies on this it is found and advised that as a consultant, you start the conversation by "asking basic and general questions, allowing whoever you're asking to say what comes to mind first, rather than asking leading questions from the beginning. Then start asking specific questions." By starting basic and drilling into specifics, you can begin to frame your questions around what your proposed solution can benefit the customer differently.

3. Active Listening

The better you are at asking questions, the less you will need to say, and the more listening you will need to do. True understanding requires active listening, which helps you absorb what is being said, and what's not being said. A large component of active listening is knowing when not to interrupt. Most of that conversation should be spent actively listening, not talking. Leave the talking to the buyer. To improve active listening, consider these tips and techniques:

- Remove distractions (checking the phone, eating, looking at another person, or viewing outside)

- Take notes (the detail the better, but try to note every point customer says)

- Do not simply wait to talk (this happens with most of us. When we get any important point, we try to interrupt, or we wait to ask the question on that point. This leads to blocking your listening on other points said thereafter)

- Never interrupt (This disturbs the flow of the speaker. And at times he may miss an important point that he was about to say)

- Act like the buyer is the only person in the world (Give the customer utmost importance. This makes him feel comfortable to disclose all his pain points)

- Do not be like a statue while listening but respond with eye contact, nodding your head, and by using words of acknowledgment such as "OK", "Right", "True", "Oh" etc.)

- When the customer has finished his sentence and you have a point to ask, then give a pause and ask short clarifying questions, such as "Can you expand on this" and "What do you mean by that"

- Summarize your understanding either at the end or when the customer has finished answering one question. For example: "If I have understood correctly, you are saying that…".

If you practice active listening, you will learn more, but talk less. I mentioned "customers" and "Client'. They need not be always the external ones who pay for the project. The client can be internal such as the project manager, the project in-charge who is giving you the task of solving the client's problem.

4. Inform or advise or provide a proposed solution

Advise on the solution that can solve a customer problem and benefit him. Provide the approach to a solution by which the problem can be solved. Give reasons on how the solution is better and how the solution can get the best return on the investment.

5. Closure

Closure can be just a formality but is especially important. It must be done very carefully so that both customers and consultants are on the same page. The agreements must be signed with all terms and conditions mentioned. Closing a deal does not usually happen all at once. The customer may need to discuss your solution with his team for final input. They may need to have a conversation with their decision authority to determine if a consultant's solution is in line with their business strategy.

This should not take much time if the customer is convinced of your solution discussed earlier. At times due to customer's priority or financial adjustments, it can take time. Do not rush with the customer to close the deal. It may end your relationship or may take your relationship to a different angle. Patience is the key. Once the agreement is signed, do proper communication on execution updates, follow-ups after project closure, and be in contact with the customer for the long term.

> "People don't care about your business. They care about their problems. Be the solution that they are looking for"
>
> – Melonie Dodaro

I had my doubts about the product selling approach, services selling approach, transactional selling, and consultative selling approach. I went to Dev's residence and on a cup of coffee discussion, I requested him to clear my doubt.

It was a Sunday afternoon, Dev was with his son, who was making a drawing. After chatting for few minutes about family and work, I asked "is consultative selling is better than transactional selling."

Dev responded and said, "It depends on the situation, customer need, buyer's understanding of his need". As always, Dev continued explaining this with his experience.

"Let me explain to you this. Once I and my son went to a book stationary shop. I needed a black pen and my son needed a pencil for his drawing. I asked the shopkeeper for a microtip black color gel pen. Here, as a buyer, I am clear about what I need. As a shopkeeper, he has to push his product where can make a good profit, he started showing the pens with the same specification. I use one specific brand as I feel comfortable with the grip in my fingers. But he was pushing a little higher priced pen with the same specification. This is transactional selling. Because the shopkeeper is only focused on his product. After finalizing the pen, I asked him to give a dark lead pencil for my son. To this started conversation with my son.

"Hi, are you learning the art, or is it for your school project work"

"I learn art in an art academy" My son replied.

"Very good boy. So, what kind of drawing you like to make?" He continued his questions

"I like pencil sketching, especially landscape art". My son also felt comfortable and started sharing his details.

"That is wonderful. Do you use, glossy paper art or are you making in the sketchbook that is given by the academy"? The shopkeeper further investigated.

"Yes, I am using the sketchbook given in the academy and during holidays, I use the A0 size drawing sheets like this (pointing towards the sheet that was kept in one corner of the shop)." My son described his drawing.

At this point, the shopkeeper was clear about my son's requirement and he went to one of the shelves and got a box of pencils. He said to me, "Sir, for your son, these pencils will suit best for his sketching work. These are sets of pencils with different types of shades. It has light to dark shades, and fine to bold tips. With this, he will be able to make the best sketches. There are different types in this, which are set of three pencils to set of ten. I would suggest, for his age and type of drawing he makes, the set of three will be best suited."

This is consultative selling. Here buyer is given importance. The product was not pushed (the shopkeeper could have pushed the ten set pencils), but the problem was solved.

"I think, I could able to make you understand and clarify your doubt. Let me give you some distinguishing properties of transactional and consultative selling", Dev said to me.

There are nine differentiating approaches between transactional and consultative sales.

1. Focus
    a. In transactional selling, the salesperson talks about the product
    b. In consultative selling, the consultant talks about the prospect
2. Assumption
    a. In transactional selling, the salesperson assumes that every prospect needs the product

b. In consultative selling, the consultant tries to find out if the prospect needs the product

3. Selling priority

    a. In transactional selling, the salesperson tries to sell the product to every prospect

    b. A consultant does market research to find a prospect who is a good fit for the product in consultative selling

4. Selling approach

    a. The salesperson tries to sell at the first step and keeps trying to sell at every sales step he progresses in transactional selling

    b. In consultative selling, the consultant tries to build confidence and sells the next step

5. Communication

    a. The salesperson does most of the talking in transaction selling (about products and their specifications)

    b. In consultative selling, the customer does most of the talking (based on the question asked by the consultant or salesperson)

6. Interest building

    a. In transaction selling, the salesperson talks about only the product and tries to make the product interesting

    b. In consultative selling approach, the consultant talks about the solution to the problem, its benefits, ROI, and previous examples to make the solution interesting

7. Value

    a. In a transactional sale, the value lies within the product and price becomes the primary selection criteria.

    b. In a consultative sale, the salesperson creates value for the customer. VALUE is the difference between BENEFITS and COST.

8. Leadership thought

    a. Transactional sales focus on achieving sales/revenue target

    b. Consultative sale focuses on solving client's problem and building long term relationship

9. Rewards and recognition

    a. In the transactional sale approach, rewards are on the number of sales and revenue earned

    b. In consultative sale approach, the team celebrates customer success and new solution development

The last three points are mainly on the leadership on how he takes the sales approach. This can change consultative sales into transactional sales and vice versa. If a consultant is developing a project with a client, the leader can ask him to close the deal at the earliest so that revenue can be earned, and the team can be engaged in the project. This is quite common in the geospatial sector. By this most of the time, with revenue-focused, it leads to low volume low-value projects and misses high-value long term projects.

The motivation of the consultant is also lost in creating value for the client. A consultant is always motivated by the success of the customer and by the value he creates for the customer. So that the relationship can bring many more projects to the company.

Dev went to the whiteboard that was hanged on the wall. Some mathematics calculations were written on the board. I guessed that might be his son's work. He erased everything and wrote, "*Time spent with a client*" on the top. He made this figure (as given below) that explained the time spent with a client on the transactional and consultative approach of selling. He says, "this picture can give a complete understanding of geospatial projects where these approaches are used. It applies in most of the sectors. I have observed in my long career in the geospatial agriculture sector that, immediately after the first meeting is done with the client, the salesperson submits a proposal within a couple of days. He starts his follow-up from there onwards. There go multiple iterations on the scope which makes the revision in prices and it goes on for a long time".

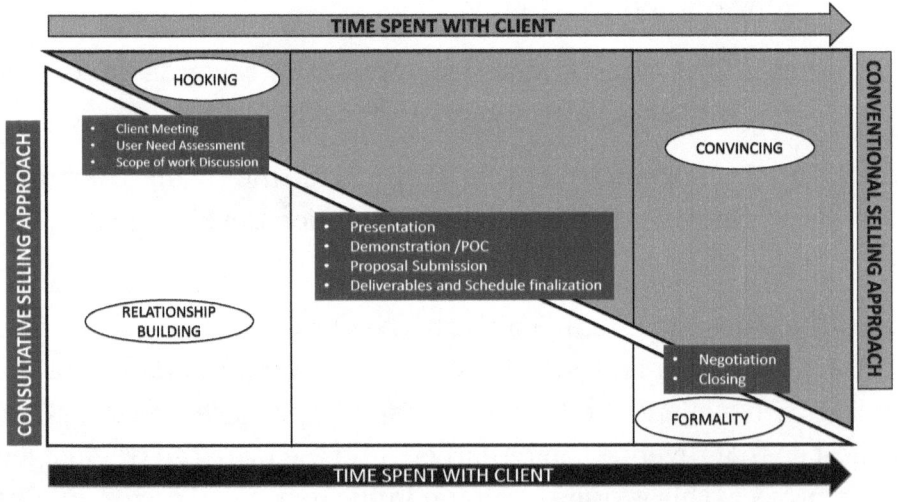

"If the consultative sales approach is followed systematically, then financial proposal becomes just a formality to be done between the customer and service provider. Once again, I say, in consultative selling, technical skills and patience is more important"

> "*Care enough to create value for customers. If you get that part right, then selling is easy*"

A case study of Consulting Approach: Consulting in Food Processing Industry

This is an incident about a couple of years before when Dev met the CEO of a mid-size company that is fast expanding its business in different sectors in India and Africa. They have multiple products sold in the Indian and international markets. The latest venture for this company is in the Agriculture sector. This company invested in starting up a food processing unit. They were clear in their goal of bringing a consumable product in the market which has good demand in both rural and urban consumer segments. Since they had funds available to be invested, they acquired a large piece of land. Some lands were purchased, and some were taken on lease. The land has a mixed land use pattern. It had agricultural lands, cultivable wastelands, a large patch of scrub forest areas, and small water bodies. This patch of land was in a remote location and far from the town. They initially cleared some part of the land in the center and closer to a stream where the processing factory was planned to be constructed. They laid road from the main highway to their factory construction site. After this, they hired a construction company and started building the processing unit. The construction part went on for about a year and a half. About 60% of the construction work was done. It was expected to get completed in another six to eight months.

It was at a dinner party of a common friend, where the Chief executive officer of this company Mr. Ashish met with Dev. The common friend introduced Dev as an Agriculture expert to Mr. Ashish. He gave a brief about Mr. Ashish as CEO who looks after business in Central Africa and he presently stays with his family in Nairobi, Kenya. He came to India for this new venture. Since this was an agriculture venture, he thought it will be of some help to both and he left to attend to other guests after introducing them.

The conversation between Mr. Ashish and Mr. Dev went like this...

Ashish: "Hello, Mr. Dev, I am Ashish from ABC Company".

Dev: "Hello Mr. Ashish. How are you and How is everything in business going on?"

Ashish: "Oh Yes Mr. Dev, everything is fine. I am a bit busy nowadays as we have invested in the Agriculture business". He gave his visiting card to Dev

Dev: "Thank you. I have heard about your company. But never heard of it in Agriculture sector"

Ashish: "That is true, Mr. Dev. We are into manufacturing, real estate and have retail stores in major states of India. The manufacturing unit is in Nairobi, Kenya. The real estate and retail stores business is in India. This is the first time we are getting not agribusiness".

Dev: "That is wonderful Mr. Ashish. What kind of Agriculture business is it?"

"It is a food processing unit; replied Mr. Ashish. We have our retail shops where we will be adding this food product for sale. We have done our analysis and found that there is a lot of demand for this product. Hence, we started working on this".

"How far it has come Mr. Ashish?" Dev again questioned

(This is the quality of a consultant, questioning to find if he is having any problem and giving solutions. Dev is aware of the techniques of consulting)

"We have built the team for India operations, started the construction of processing facilities. The processing types of machinery have been purchased. Now it is in the final stage to get the machines fit it and tested". Ashish responded.

Listening to this Dev said. "A lot of work is done. Your team might have researched the area, climate, farmers, soil, water, and other related things?"

"You know Mr. Dev, it has been more than a year and a half now, we have been pumping money on construction of processing unit, infrastructure, and machinery. We hope it to be ready by this year-end and our product will be there in shops by the start of the new year".

After about 30 minutes of discussion, Dev realized that there is some gap in Mr. Ashish's approach. Dev requested Mr. Ashish for asking few more questions related to his business which will benefit him. And invited for a meeting over a coffee the next morning. Initially, Mr. Ashish hesitated and thought in his mind that, Mr. Dev is a subject matter expert, and how is he going to help in business. Since he was going to be in the town for a couple of days, Mr. Ashish decided to continue the discussion.

The next morning in the coffee shop at 8 AM

Dev reached the decided place by 7:55 AM and was waiting for Mr. Ashish. He got a message on his phone from Mr. Ashish that he is getting ready and will be there in a couple of minutes. It was the same hotel where Mr. Ashish was staying.

Meanwhile, Dev was going through the menu card on the varieties of coffee being served in the restaurant. A piece of slow music was playing in the background, that was not noisy and even not that low too. He went to the garden just outside the restaurant to look at the flowers and nicely timed hedgerows. As he was looking deep into the flowers, he heard a voice from behind………. Good Morning Mr. Dev.

"Good Morning Mr. Ashish. How was your night? Hope you had good sleep in our state". Asked Dev.

Both ordered their coffee and went to the garden to discuss while walking. Dev started the conversation.

"Mr. Ashish, you have given me details about your new project. I have understood its current stage and have done my analysis. I have a few observations and questions which I would like to put to you".

The coffee arrived and Mr. Ashish said, please go-ahead Mr. Dev.

"Mr. Ashish, as you mentioned that about 100 to 150 metric tons of fruits will be crushed daily in the factory. Have you finalized the areas from where these fruits will be procured?"

"No……Yes. We can procure it from the farmers". Mr. Ashish said

"Mr. Ashish, have you done any survey, whether that crop is grown in that region? If yes then where, how much is the area, and what is the production and why will farmer sell to you if he has his buyer fixed for last many years".

"Mr. Ashish, you may require having some arrangement with farmers to get their products to your factory. As your product is a processed food, it requires a good quality fruit of a specific variety. Have you found if farmers grow that variety? If not, then what is the plan".

"Mr. Ashish, you have been spending money on the construction of the processing unit which is fine. But simultaneously, if the large piece of land surrounding the factory is cleared and converted into that fruit cultivation then you can have your raw material available. Since crop requires sometimes to grow, it will be ready by the time your factory is ready. This will not make your factory idle till finding the raw material".

"Mr. Ashish these are few things which I thought there is a gap, so I mentioned. It is your take now".

Mr. Ashish was silent for some time and then he got up went to the restaurant counter and ordered another round of coffee for both. He came back to the place and said, Mr. Dev, to be honest, I did not give importance to all these. Now I realize that I was going to do a mistake and would have landed into trouble.

"Mr. Dev Let me know how we plan all this?"

(This is the point where a subject matter expert can transform himself into a consultant. Convert the opportunity into business. Usually, at this stage, the expert will help him out with creating a plan and giving advice as and *when he is been called. It will so happen that, Mr. Ashish will be out of the picture and some managers will start interacting and the expert will be busy providing service as a charity. The company will nicely treat, pay for his ticket whenever he is traveling to their unit, put him in a guest house with nice food, etc. But there will not be any fee or agreement done. Even if the fee is paid, it will not be with format agreement but as an allowance).*

Would you be interested to know what Dev did?

Dev said, "do not worry Mr. Ashish. Just give me a couple of days, and I will submit my proposal on how all the raw material production and procurement planning can be done for effectively running the processing unit".

The next day, Dev submitted a brief conceptual note describing the scope of work, broad activities, and type of deliverables. Once both agreed to the scope of work with some minor refinements on deliverables, Dev submitted the proposal two days after the concept note was submitted. This proposal now had a detailed scope of work, approach, methodology, deliverables, support required, and project schedule and technical terms and conditions. He did not do the sales at the first step. This is how a consultant works. First, he identifies the problem, analyses the depth of the problem, works on a solution, and then submits the proposal. Once the proposed scope of work is finalized and agreed by both the end, the financial proposal is submitted. The financial proposal becomes just a formality to close the paperwork. This follows execution.

> *"Results happen over time, not overnight. Work hard, stay consistent and be patient"*

Consulting project on Agriculture food processing unit development

It was a couple of weeks gone after Mr. Ashish and Mr. Dev's meeting. Dev sent an email to Mr. Ashish enquiring about his work. Dev has this quality of follow-up with clients so as keep the client engaged in the discussion.

Dev received an email from Mr. Ashish stating that he would like to hire his services for creating the crop development and procurement plan for the processing unit.

They had few emails exchanged about availability, fees, working models, etc. The scope of work was finalized, and an agreement was sent to Dev for the assignment.

Dev chooses for solo consulting with the targeted date of deliverables. He must deliver the plan first then later to support in implementation. Till the delivery of the plan document, he chooses solo consulting. He had the advantage to work from home or any place he wishes to.

It was three months assignment and after the deadline, Dev visited the company site for the plan presentation. The site was far from the city. They had sent a pickup vehicle for him at the airport. On that day he was booked in a luxurious hotel near the airport.

The moment he reached the hotel room, he gets a call from Mr. Ashish on welcoming him to town and fixing time for the next day's meeting. The time was fixed for 9 AM.

The next day company vehicle arrives at the hotel at 8 AM to pick up Dev. He was ready after having his breakfast with a laptop bag and was waiting in the lobby. Dev got into the vehicle and started for the site. He asked the driver about the distance and time to reach the place. He says it will take about 45 to 50 minutes to reach the site.

Dev was reading a news article and after 20 minutes when they crossed the city limit, he started looking at the fields outside. He was looking at the landscape, people and all that was crossing them.

At around 8:50 AM they reached the site. The driver took him to a guest room next to the meeting hall. He was served with some fruit juices and bakery items. He was about to take the glass of juice, the known voice came again, Hello Mr. Dev.

They shook hands and this time it was a warmer handshake as they now knew each other.

Mr. Ashish said let us go to the meeting room and we will discuss it there. Both took juice glass and picked some biscuits and entered the meeting room.

After 5 minutes and exactly at 9 AM two other gentlemen joined them in the meeting. One of them was their chief operating officer and the other was their chief financial officer.

After the introduction, Dev started his talk. He said to all that, he would like to make the presentation more information so that we can discuss in between any point that comes to mind. This will clear all our doubts then and there itself.

Dev started the talk, "Gentlemen, we know that in about 6 to 7 months construction of processing unit and machinery testing will be completed. This means we have only 6 to 7 months to plan out input for the factory to run. Hence what I have worked out is we need two teams to work on the field. One team will work on the land area around the factory for its clearance, leveling, irrigation channeling, irrigation source creation, seed selection and procurement, other input arrangements, etc. For this, a team of an agronomist, soil conservation expert, and plant protection expert will be required. They will work from land preparation till harvest of the produce. The second team will work outside the factory area to find out farmers who are growing this crop and make them registered for the company. Once they are registered, this team should monitor them in the type of seeds they are using and the management practices they follow. The quality that is required for the product should come to the factory".

"We also need one agriculture market research expert who can research best seeds available in the region, price of the product, place where farmers sell their produce, price of produce, what are the benefits farmers get, what are

the problems faced by the farmer to sell the products and get the payment. If farmer's problem can be addressed by us, then they will give produce to us".

Listening to this both CFO and COO raised their hand to ask a question.

COO said, "it will be difficult to hire this big team and manage them throughout the year. Then we need to build a human resource department. Adding to this CFO said, this will add cost to the company, and we will have to have them in our payroll".

Dev said, "we need not worry about hiring and managing resources. For this, we can hire a consulting firm that can do all these activities. The benefit of this will be to have them only for the crop season. Their agreement can be from land preparation till the first harvest of the crop. From the second season onwards, we can develop our team to monitor crop".

"Another firm can be hired which can manage the supply of product from farmers field to factory. Factory should have a storage facility and quality team".

"We need to monitor and set the targets. For example, if the processing capacity of the unit is 100 tons per day and is planned to operate for four months then about 15000 tons of products will be required. This means if average yield per acre is 5 tons, then about 2500 acres is required".

"Alongside factory 600 acres are available with the company. The first team's target will be to develop 600 acres for crop production. We may not get the entire 600 acres for our target crop as it may not be 100% suitable. Hence the maximum we can get can be used for our crop and the rest can be used for alternate crops that can be sold to our factory staff. Some land can come under recreational purposes and some under social forestry. The second team will have to work on getting farmers registered for 2000 acres".

"Market research team can be hired on a part-time basis. They can visit sites on two days a weekly basis and produce the report by end of every month. Freshers or student interns can be hired for this purpose".

Mr. Ashish got in and said "yes, this looks feasible to optimize our cost and time for managing resources. This way we can concentrate on construction and machinery work. Once the raw material starts coming it, we can focus on the packaging, distribution, and marketing"

Dev mentioned next that, "everything may not work smoothly as we plan. Hence, we need to ready for challenges. For example, the 600 acres around may not be highly suitable for the crop hence some investment may go in to develop land to bring the less suitable land into a suitable category. Similarly, all 2000 acres farmers registered with us may not give the product to us. They may go to another party as well. Hence, we should be ready for an additional 500 acres farmers".

All three at the time said, "yes that is true, we need to be prepared for risks and challenges".

This way the meeting went till lunch and then after lunch, it continued till the end of the day.

At night Mr. Ashish invited Dev for dinner. During the dinner, he mentioned that "the plan is good but I need your help in monitoring the plan and activities going on till work is understood by all the team".

Dev agrees but says he can take up the part-time assignment and will plan to visit one day a week to look at the progress and guide the team accordingly.

Dev first submitted the scope of work that he was going to execute. There were some changes suggested by Mr. Ashish in the scope of work. The scope was re-submitted and on getting confirmation Dev submitted the project activity schedule, roles and responsibility sheet, and support that will be required from ABC company. This took about 6 to 7 calls between them and about a dozen of email exchanges. Once these were finalized, Dev submitted his financial proposal. In the next email itself, the financial and project proposal was accepted. The agreement process was initiated.

Dev gets another long-term part-time consulting assignment.

> *"If you want to build a long-term successful enterprise, you can't focus on **closing the sale**. You have to focus on **opening the relationship**"*

Section 4

Engage

Recognize Uncover Learn <u>Engage</u> Secure

Chapter 7

Nine Motives to Become Geospatial Consultant

"In the business world, everyone is paid in two coins: cash and experience. Take the experience first; the cash will come later."

– Harold Geneen

Before we get into the reasons for "why anyone wants to/should become a consultant", let us understand the geospatial industry. This industry is dominated by service providing companies who use GIS technology to create maps and data for the users. These users are mainly the telecommunication sector, mining sector, urban development organizations, disaster management organization, agriculture, forestry, and others. The second category of companies in the geospatial industry is product development companies, who develop applications and software such as GIS mapping software, Image processing software, GPS instruments, field survey apps, drone image processing applications, and software, etc. These are the new generation companies that have come up recently over 6 to 8 years from now. The third category in the geospatial industry is government ministries having GIS unit in their departments. Most of these GIS units can be found in urban development, irrigation planning, water resources, forestry, agriculture research institutes, etc.

To define the geospatial agriculture sector, these are the companies that provide services to the agriculture industry, government agriculture departments, and support other sectors where agriculture data plays important role in their decision-making processes.

In the geospatial agriculture sector, the professionals start their career from as an executive, to senior executive then get into a managerial role and go to an administrative role. Some professionals shift their domain to other sectors such as urban or telecommunication where the volume and value of the project are huge. The other reason being from the non-agriculture domain so they can fit in any sector. Whereas few individuals do not want to just get fit in but would like to grow by their skills, creativity, knowledge, etc.

Each year, some professionals are getting attracted to the consulting profession. Some professionals chose to pursue a life-long dream of independence, freedom, and financial success. Others run away from jobs and situations in hope of finding something better. The reason for this is because, Consulting provides exceptional opportunities to work on the project you like, progress quickly in your career, collaborate with talented people, and travel to new places. Some of the benefits of consulting are compensation, learning, network, and new opportunities. But most of them are not able to get into and continue to work in their existing profession.

The other reason why one should become a consultant is to fill the gap between the client's needs and the service provider's understanding. Currently, in the geospatial agriculture sector, most of the user needs assessment is done by a salesperson who will be looking after-sales of all sectors. Hence for him, all projects are the same, be it telecommunication, mining, agriculture, or urban planning. His job is to find the client and explain what the company does in the first step. In the next step, when any prospective client submits his requirements, the sales get active with the bidding team to submit the proposal as per the email sent by the client. In that proposal, all the promises will be made on the timeline, budget deliverables, etc. In the next step, he will negotiate with the client and close the deal to meet his target. The real problem will arise when a project comes for execution. Where it will be found that the requirement and proposed deliverable has no match. I am telling this as an example that happens most often. Some of the companies have improved in this by involving a technical person in proposal making and client interactions. This is the reason; one should have a consulting mindset or attitude so that the need can be understood, and the best solution can be provided that can benefit both the user and the service provider in the long run. The consultative sales approach is explained in one of the later chapters.

In an earlier chapter, we have explained the myths that stop these individuals to become consultants and start helping others with a purpose. In this section, we will discuss the nine reasons for individuals to become a consultant in detail.

The nine reasons are divided into two categories. The first one about the people who can become a consultant and the second one is the situation that can make these individuals become a consultant.

Individuals who can/should become a consultant

Out of the nine reasons given below, you may be falling in any one category or you may have a combination of two or more reasons together. If you are falling in this category, then you must get into consulting rather than dragging into current work that you do not like or shifting the job for the sake of earning.

1. Specialists or experienced professionals:

In general, the first category of a professional look for consulting after they have spent many years in the industry and now feel like giving back to society with a price. The second category in this are professional who are either about to retire or who has retired will look for consulting to keep himself/herself busy and keep earning. The third category in this is experienced professionals who have spent many years in the industry and is now in a senior management position but is vulnerable. Anytime his position will be replaced by some young professional at a low salary.

To be a geospatial agriculture consultant, one needs to be experienced in working on agriculture projects using remote sensing and GIS technique. This individual must have experience in executing a minimum of three to four projects for clients. This is essential for the expert to understand the project requirements, the inputs that can be used to solve the client's problem, the time and resources required for meeting the project requirements, etc. Hence these are a specific category of individuals. They can be agriculture or non-agriculture graduates but should have experience in handling projects using geospatial techniques.

2. Anyone looking for a career change:

These are the second set of individuals who are in the job for the sake of monthly income. These people are not happy and satisfied either with the work or with the monthly package. Hence, they look for assignments as additional income. In this group, there is another category who is also working for monthly income but is not able to spend time on his passion.

In geospatial agriculture, this category of individuals can be found in many. The reason could be

- a. "not happy with the boss, because of work he is assigned is out of his domain area"
- b. "not being listened on his/her subject-based advice on the project"
- c. "not being given value for his contribution on the project"

d. "being an agriculture expert and not been allowed to interact with client team"

   e. "not being paid well"

3. Individuals with some challenges or limitations:

This is the group where individuals become a consultant because of their need. They have some limitations by which they cannot take up any job. Hence, they prefer to work as a consultant at their own pace and time.

The first category in this are individuals who must take care of their family (elderly parents, or infants, or relatives needing medical attention). They would prefer to work from home on a task completion basis. This means they can spend their own time to complete the task and need not have to work like 9 AM to 5 PM or during any office hours.

The second category in this group is either fired from a job or who are forced to leave because of company closure. There could be any reason. He or she is unemployed. He/she look for short-term assignments and uses his/her skills and then becomes consultants.

The third category is individuals who have medical issues. Such as pregnant women, differently-abled individuals, individuals with some health issues. They have difficulties in commuting between office and home or sitting in one place for long hours. They would prefer to work at their convenience place. This makes them take up consultancy.

The fourth category is individuals who do not have any challenges but have some limitations of working for any boss. This group prefers to be on their own, and take-up assignments that they can deliver at ease. They need not have to prove anyone on their performance.

If an individual falls in any of the category mentioned above and has experience of working agriculture-based projects for some years or have executed multiple agriculture projects using remote sensing and GIS technique can become a consultant.

4. Freshers or new graduates:

These are a group of individuals who are hired directly from their college or immediately after passing out from college based on their skills, dissertation work, and marks obtained. These individuals will then be given some on-job training and will be put into the project as a consultant either on the client site or in-house. In today's business, start-up companies are established companies looking for young and fresh talents as consultants.

These are of two types:

- o Contract workers: hired for the project-to-project contract.
- o Project-based staff: hired for the project and then will be on the bench when no related project

These are especially important groups of people who should take up consulting. Being fresher, they should develop a consulting mindset. This will help in executing the project, not as part of the delivery to the client but think of work as a problem-solving work. These are the people who will be working on the project during the contract and will be developing skills or learning new techniques during the non-project time. The interest can be developed right from the beginning of a career.

Dev (Geospatial Agriculture consultant) prefers to train freshers on consulting in agriculture with geospatial technology. For them, Dev has customized training modules to teach the technique as well as a conceptual approach and consultative approach to handle the client's needs.

Why an individual wants to become a Consultant

There is another set of individuals who want to become consultants, who have some reason to take up consulting. This can be an individual from anyone from the category mentioned above. The reasons could be any of the following

5. Having flexibility and true freedom:

While most of the GIS experts working in the agriculture area are stuck in rush-hour traffic. These individuals would like to work on their schedule but are not allowed to due to policies and rules of the human resources department. They can set their hours so that they can spend more time with friends and family. In geospatial agriculture, the work is about the input (satellite images, secondary data of field points, and reference maps), analysis to be done in image processing software and GIS software, and finally output to be generated for the client. This can be done from any place and at any time duration of the day. Today we are in the digital world, where we can have access to any system, we can have video calls, share screens, and perform with high productivity. These sets of people need hand-holding from a coach or mentor on starting consulting. In one of the later chapter steps to become a consultant is explained in detail.

6. Work to reach your full potential:

These are individuals who love to work with new opportunities that can bring out the best in them. But are given the opportunity and are kept engaged in other project activities. They are passionate about doing something that most people regret not doing. Dev, in the later stage of his working career, was very enthusiastic about working with a client, solving problems, developing new projects that can benefit the company, and funding agency. He used to execute the agriculture projects and in addition to that was mostly kept engaged by his company on human resources and administrative activities. He used to look after the travel bills, attendance, etc. Whereas he was interested in developing more automated solutions based on the concepts he had. He also wanted to utilize the non-productive time on training the team on agriculture concepts. This is the time when he decided to get into consulting so that he can have a defined role to play.

7. Become your boss:

These are individuals who do not like to work under any superior. Once they are consultants, they do not have to answer to anyone. They are not forced to do anything that they do not want to do. They hate corporate politics. And they are the leader of their destiny.

One of the incidences of Dev's career. It was his earlier days when he had a couple of years of experience in agriculture projects and was promoted to lead a small team of GIS experts. Dev being from agriculture professional and having GIS experience, studied the project he was going to handle, and was discussing with his team for the best and quick GIS approach to obtain a result. As an agriculture professional he has explained the output that client desires. Now the action item was to get a quick technique to follow during the project execution. The team members were excited and started working on the different approaches that can be used. At this moment Dev was called by his reporting manager who said *"Dev, do not use your brain, just follow the project specifications (operating manual) that we have been following in other projects. If it is taking time, then ask the team to work late hours and complete the job. If required let them work the whole night. Ask them to work day and night till the results are ready for shipment."* In that project, the team members worked for non-stop 120 hours by taking only short naps at night and few breaks to fresh-up. Although the work was done and submitted to the client on time.

Dev never had a liking towards his reporting manager then. Later on, when Dev started leading the team in his career he realized, the work should be done smartly with analytical capabilities in GIS and if the work takes time then it should be discussed with the client.

8. Nature of the work:

Consulting is a helpful process that adds value to an organization. The nature of the process, from assessment, conceptualization, analysis, and solutions is all exciting work. It is always challenging and self-fulfilling. This becomes difficult when the potential of a geospatial agriculture expert having expertise in handling various kinds of agriculture requirements does not match with organization goals.

Let us understand this in-depth from Dev's experience. Dev has experience executing projects for seed companies, fertilizer companies, agriculture commodity trading companies, crop insurance organizations, investors in Africa, research organizations, and projects from multilateral funding agencies. At one point in his career, he joined a startup to build their agriculture business unit. With the help of a salesperson, he was able to get projects from seed companies and trading organizations. These projects were season based to generate crop intelligence reports and can be executed quickly. The work became monotonous and the team was set to execute it without much technical input required. Dev worked with the sales team to diversify and created opportunities for an international client on agriculture-based livelihood development and crop productivity improvement projects. The project was developed as long term and highly valued. But the management did not agree to take this project as this needs more consulting mind involvement and does not have any automation. Similarly, in another incident, Dev developed the project with a government agriculture research organization where the work involved, training, capacity building, and executing in partnership with the research organization team on cropping pattern change analysis of a sub-district that was adopted by this organization. This required about the past fifteen years of data analysis and creating a land-use perspective plan for the coming seasons. For this also, the management did not give any agreement. They asked Dev to focus on crop intelligence report automation. Dev used to argue with his mentor friend Dr. Priya that he will leave the geospatial sector and get into field-based agriculture projects in some other organization. Dr. Priya has many times convinced him not to leave his niche area where he has spent years and years. And will always guide him to continue so that he can pass on the knowledge to his team members, freshers and make them experts.

9. Having the liberty to choose your client and projects you like:

This is one of the good parts of consulting that a consultant is never forced to work with certain people or on certain projects. He/She can choose who you want to work with, and which type of project you want to work on. In today's scenario, an individual having expertise in GIS and Image processing will be asked to work in any project be it Agriculture, urban, water resources, disaster, insurance, etc. In such cases, the individual is using his/her skills to complete the project but is not developing his expertise in any specific sector to solve the problem of the client. The reason for this is being an employee, one can use his skills but not the expertise or experience.

Once an employee has a consulting mindset and creates value in the company then he can position well himself/herself in the organization for specific kinds of projects. If he/she is an external consultant then he/she can choose to work on the project where value can be added, the problem of the client can be solved with benefits and future relations can be built.

Once you get into consulting then you do not have to fight for salary raise that happens only at a fixed timeline. They are free to choose how much they want to earn. They can raise or change the price whenever they want, depending on the client or project. As a Geospatial Agriculture Consultant (External) or Geospatial Agriculture expert (within the organization), one can understand the purpose of client requirements, conceptualize the project, prepare the working plan and execute in the best way to solve client's problem.

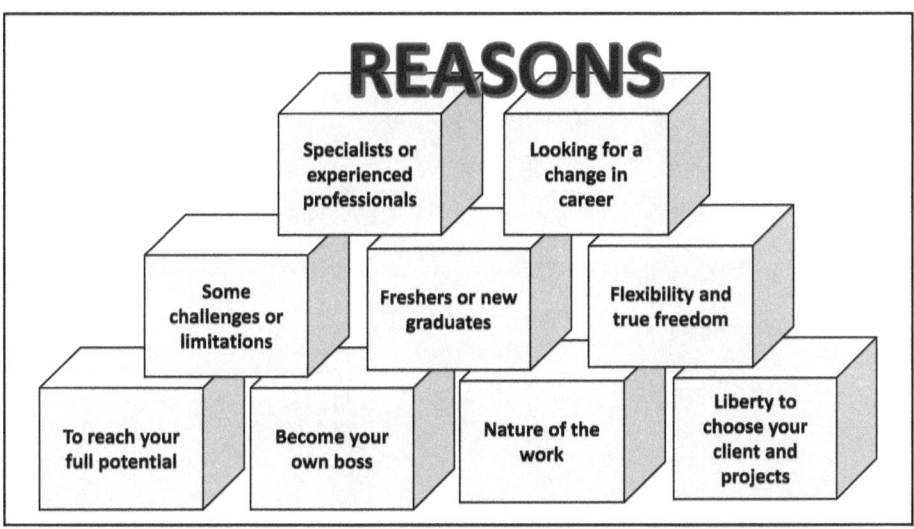

Although Dev suggests to every professional that "Consulting is not a position but a thought process". Before anyone is taking into consulting, they must ask themselves two questions.

Q1: Can you solve the problem that your client has?

Q2: Can you lead (the project or the team or the discussion or the concept or anything that is required to solve the problem)

"The man who will use his skill and constructive imagination to see how much he can give for a dollar, instead of how little he can give for a dollar, is bound to succeed"

– Henry Ford

Chapter 8

Nine Forms of Consultancy and Consulting Business

"Hard work in the wrong place equals to no work but suffering and struggling

Hard work in the right place equals to ease, rest, and progressive success

Be wise, wisdom is the principal thing and not your might"

– Jolene Quotes

Now that we have discovered that, to become an authority in geospatial agriculture, one must recognize his potential and shift his thinking to consulting mindset, which is nothing but relationship building and problem-solving. We have also cleared the myths that an individual carries about consulting and studies the reasons for becoming a consultant. Now when these things are clear there will be some more questions that arise such as, do consultants work alone, do they work for someone, do they have a team, do they only provide service or do they sell a product, can they have flexibility in working, can they have fewer working hours, so on and on. In this chapter, we will investigate the types of consulting that an expert can choose based on his level of skills, years of experience, and current situation.

Often professionals spend most of their time and substantial money on setting up an office, business cards, website, letterheads, laptops, furniture, etc., before getting into consulting profession/business. Whereas the first and most vital step in starting a consulting business is to first, define your goal. Bring clarity on what you want to be. Then work on your core strength which is called a unique selling proposition. Followed by this define your market and customer segment. In a later chapter, all these steps to become a consultant are explained in detail.

Once an individual starts executing consulting assignments, he/she thinks of starting a business in consulting. There are different types of consulting business. These are explained below paragraphs. In this section, we will understand the types of working in consulting and types of consulting business that can be considered by a geospatial (agriculture) expert.

There are typically nine types of Consulting

1. Sector Specific Consulting

In sector-specific consulting, you are confined to one sector say Agriculture. Any problem at the client end, related to agriculture then specialized expert solves the problem. For example, if the client is having a problem related to soils, then the soil science consultant is hired, if the problem is related to pests and diseases, then an entomology or plant pathology consultant is deployed. If post-harvest and marketing related problems, then an agribusiness consultant can be deployed. In the GIS industry, a geospatial agriculture consultant plays an especially important role as he/she is a sector-specific consultant who can understand the problem of the client and define the execution model for the GIS team. He may not be suitable in another sector such as urban planning, mineral exploration, telecommunication but he is unbelievably valuable in agriculture-based projects. He/she will be able to handle, problems of seed companies, trading groups, research organizations, the insurance sector, etc.

2. Solution Specific Consulting

Solution-specific consulting is where one core problem is identified, and a solution related to that problem is solved. The consultant or consulting form develops a solution for that problem and sell it to multiple clients having similar problems. A lot of GIS companies are into this where crop acreage reporting and crop health monitoring has been customized and automatized. The advantage in this is the solution can be customized after some time, as it is a repetitive job. For example, crop acreage and crop health monitoring, the process of image processing are the same, the analysis is the same the indices used are more or less the same. Due to repetitive work, the efficiency and accuracy increase. Hence major part of the works gets automated and a small portion of work is where the consultant's intervention will be required such as identification of crops to be classified. The benefit of such a model is scalability. It has a high potential to scale to multiple clients and at multiple geographies. The disadvantage competes with other companies. A similar solution if exist in the market then the value goes down. The value increases if the diversified solutions are developed. For example, solution for the crop insurance sector, solution for the land development sector, solution for crop productivity improvement projects, etc.

3. Consulting by yourself

This is a type of consulting model in which the consultant is the owner, and he/she is in "On your Own" mode. This type of consulting is also known as "Solo Consulting". In this, the consultant is the brand of the business. This type of consultant is hired by any client looking at his/her skills and experience. For example, if a client has to generate crop intelligence information for maize at a country level using satellite images, then they will hire an expert who has done similar works for multiple clients and who has an idea on the type of reports to be generated.

The consultant can hire some employees but only as assistants. As per the example given above that is maize crop intelligence information at the country level, the database creation analysis becomes a voluminous task if time is short. In such a case, the consultant can take the support of freelancing GIS experts to generate the input data for him/her. He/She can work on the analysis and reporting part and be the client's face. In solo consulting, the consultant does everything viz., project execution, sales, marketing, billing, accounting, purchases, and maintenance of assets. In this, the work is more customized, the volume of work is less but the value of an assignment is remarkably high.

The benefit of the Solo/independent model of consulting business is, it is always lean and the profit margin is high. The other benefit is the nature of work is flexible as you can set up your time and place of work. The obstacle in the solo/independent consulting business model is, at times it becomes hard to execute, do sales and marketing. Since the consultant is the brand, he/she cannot sub-contract the work to anyone which client may not like. The most difficult part of solo consulting is if you stop working then the earnings also stop.

4. Consulting Firm

The firm model of consulting is like any other registered company with a defined structure. In this either consultant himself/herself registers a company, hires employees to support, and takes an assignment in the company name. Or, it is like any other company where they hire consultants and associates to do the task. These consulting firms will have a junior and senior level of consultants. Sometimes, if the project demand (non-disclosure of end user's information), then this type of firm deploys consultants to companies on deputation also.

In the firm model, the owner spends most of his time in sales, marketing, business development, strategy making, and administrative activities. The consultants are the face to clients. Consultants do the execution. Consultants are assigned projects or deployed to the client site based on the project requirement, the budget of the project, and expertise available with the firm.

The advantage of a firm-based model is more work can be taken. The firm is the brand. More consultants can be added if the work increases. Client interaction and client management work reduces for the owner.

The disadvantage of the firm model is in the low-profit margin. The profit is the amount left after paying to consulting experts and other support staff including office expenses. Hence more clients, more projects, and high-value projects are beneficial for the firm mode of consulting. Another difficulty for a consultant in consulting form is his role. He/she may be working as a consultant but are like company employees with less freedom of work and less flexibility.

5. Full-Time Consulting

These are professionals with specialized expertise. They have multitasking skills where they have the capability and capacity to handle projects. They work full time with any firm or organization. They spend time like an employee but are not employed by the organization. The agreement of consultancy is reviewed and renewed by the firm on annual basis.

In the agriculture sector, there are organizations like Consultative Group of International agriculture research, world bank, food, and agriculture organization, and other similar organization which hire consultants as full time. These organizations work on large volumes, high-value projects like country-level planning policy designing, regional level monitoring and evaluation studies, etc, where different types of experts are required for fulltime. Such a project will have multiple domain experts and having part-time may not work out with time for all.

There are many private sectors when they bid for long-term government projects, they look to hire domain experts and consultants to work fulltime for a year or two with them.

This is up to consultants to choose the type of consulting he is comfortable with. Normally the fees are high for full-time consultants.

6. Part-Time Consulting

These are flexible workers with less specialized skills. They work only on a specific task of the project. If a project has multiple tasks and deliverables, then part-time consultants are hired to work on a specific task to complete the assignment. They may not be required full time by the organization but are required only when their role comes while executing the assignment. Organizations like, CGIAR, FAO, WB, CIMMYT, seed companies, fertilizer companies, services sector GIS companies, product development companies hire part-time consultants. A lot of startup companies who have limited hire part-time consultant on a task basis.

These consultants work on selected days in a week. They have multiple clients to work for. Their fees are slightly lower but when added for multiple clients is becomes significantly higher than any full-time employed individual. The benefit is consultants can choose the type of work he is specialized at, can choose the days he is available for assignment, can also choose the place to work for.

7. Contractual Consultants

These are individuals with specialized expertise but work on a contractual basis or project to project basis. This means that they can be full-time consultants but for a shorter period. The contract can be for a month to three or four months. In case the project extends then the contractual agreement also extends if the consultant is willing to continue.

The benefit of such type of consulting is professionals can get time after the assignment to prepare for the next assignment. Can take a break for learning or for family time.

In most agriculture companies, the surveyors are hired on a contractual basis, they can be called survey consultants. Some companies hire financial consultants at the end of every year for a month or two to do the balance sheet preparation, Form C of employees, and tax filing.

8. Internal Consultant

An internal consultant is a professional who is hired to solve an organizational problem and implement solutions to improve the performance of an organization. They can be on pay role like other employees or can be on consulting fee with a standard applicable deduction of taxes. These are experts who are at the initial stage of their career gaining experience of working with project teams. They are accountable for the project tasks they are assigned and are not responsible for any other activities. However, some of the GIS companies, especially in India hire employees and designate them as a consultant looking at their domain expertise. And these so-called designated consultants work like any other employee on any kind of project that is with the company. This is not the fault of the designated consultant, but the company is unaware of the designations. The advantage of this mode of consulting is, an individual can terminate the contract as per the agreement or can discontinue the work after the agreement term is over in case he/she does not like the work.

9. External Consultant

An external consultant is a professional who has a wider perspective gained from their extensive experience with various clients, markets, and sectors and brings new ideas and best practices along to clients. The difference lies in the relationship with the client organization; internal consultants are on the payroll or limit themselves to full-time advisory within one organization.

In an organization, there can be all five types of consultants available such as internal, external, contractual, full time and part-time along with regular employees and support staff. If an individual understands the different modes of consultancy then it is easy for him to choose based on his strengths and limitations. Also based on the expertise and requirement of the project they can be hired by clients to fulfill the requirement of projects.

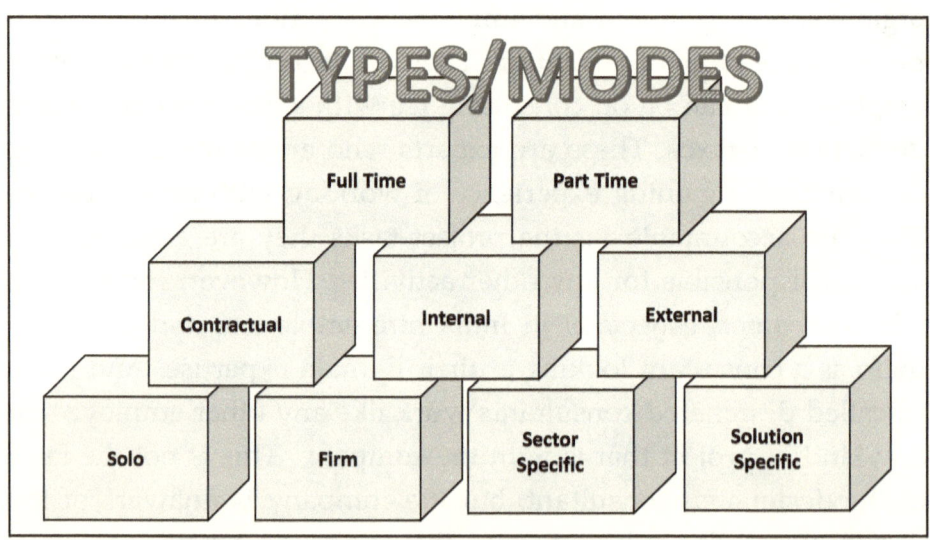

"Even though your time on the job is temporary, if you do a good enough job, your work there will last forever."

– Idowu Koyenikan

Section 5

Secure

Recognize Uncover Learn Engage <u>Secure</u>

Chapter 9

Risks and Rewards of Consulting

Till this part of the book, we have learned about the consulting mindset, the myths of consulting, skills of consulting, consultative sales approach, and modes of consulting. The transition from an employee to a consultant can be an exciting one, with the independence of work, choice of opportunities, and control over your working future. But it can also be a frightening change that brings new risks.

> *"Opportunity and risk come in pairs"*
>
> **– Bangambiki Habyarimana**

Every business, regardless of size or industry, will get into problems at some point. Sometimes companies can solve these problems in-house. Other times require help from an outside resource — a consultant or a consulting firm. Consultants are problem-solvers. This does not mean that consultants or consulting firms do not face any challenges or issues. Consulting firms have no safe choice but to tackle their risks.

A consultant's livelihood centers on providing services and advice at a professional level. As a result of the consultant's words and actions, clients alter their behavior—meaning they often hold a consultant responsible for the outcome, whether good or bad. This kind of responsibility comes with inherent risks. The risks in consulting business can vary based on your practice area. No matter whether the consulting assignment relies on one professional, small entity, or a business with several thousand professionals, all consulting firms face unique risks.

A consultant. whether is starting out or already established, if he knows the kind of challenges that may arrive will give the consultant an edge. Preparation promotes prosperity.

> *"Businesspeople need to understand the psychology of risk more than the mathematics of risk."*
>
> *– Paul Gibbons*

In this chapter, we will examine the Geospatial Agriculture environment, focusing on risks a consultant or a consulting firm must be aware of. The 9 key risks are outlined in this chapter. While there is no magical way to outright eliminate all risks in the consulting business, but awareness can mitigate the social, technical, and financial damages.

Risk No. 1: Client

The key element is consulting business is the client. If you have a client then you are growing and if you do not have a client then you are at risk. At times risks can be due to clients for who you are working. The following are some of such client's related risks.

Unhappy clients: It is a common belief that you can make anyone 100 percent satisfied. Despite a consultant's best efforts, at some point, he will face a dissatisfied client. Client dissatisfaction and consulting risk grow from many roots. Common reasons for client dissatisfactions include:

- o Missed deadlines
- o Failure to deliver on expectations

- o Cost overruns
- o Use of sub-par workers

Before a consultant initiate work with any client, he must set clear deliverables and put them in writing. Get a signed contract that details the scope of work project timeline deliverable types and format, terms of your agreement, and including costs.

The most important thing in consulting assignments is to set realistic goals and deliver on your commitments. A little more than committed is always better but less than what is committed. Client communication from the beginning is also a powerful tool to keep clients satisfied. Keep the client engaged by updating in every stage of the project.

Complicated clients: At times especially in geospatial agriculture you will find some complicated clients. They will initiate the project with a problem statement that, they are not getting reliable information from the field and they have doubts about the accuracy of published data. Once the consulting project is delivered, these clients will compare the satellite image derived results with the same information they did not believe earlier. They will start disbelieving this result also. This will create payment delays and at times non-payment by the client.

Even the clearest agreements and communications are not always enough. You may still end up with a customer who is unhappy enough to sue. How you recover from those unfortunate situations depends on your professional resilience.

Client actions: In an increasingly agile environment, intensified by rapid digital innovation, clients now expect more value, a higher quality of work, and faster delivery of solutions and services. At the same time, clients are also asking for more transparency and accountability in work delivered. Clients are monitoring the value provided by consultants with greater interest than ever before. Another factor adding to this growing scrutiny is that consulting firms no longer enjoy a monopoly on specialized knowledge. Now, much of this information is readily available online to those who are willing to research.

The other side of this action at times becomes extremely dangerous. Client's with limited internet knowledge try to confuse consultant who has years and years of working experience.

Risk No. 2: Data

Data is another most important element in consulting or any kind of business. Be it small or big business data is particularly important. There are different types of risks with data. Some of them are explained here.

Data loss: Any business can be a victim of data loss. For a consultant, it can be due to the loss of a computer system/laptop or hard drive crashing or can be due to data corruption due to a virus. In geospatial agriculture projects, some of the key data are field survey information, input satellite images, intermediary analysis files, data provided by the client as a reference. These are very critical as we know that agriculture is season based. If data lost during the season it cannot be collected again (the crop stage will be lost). But if your consulting business stores data on your servers, the consequences of a data loss can be resolved. Best practice to prevent data loss can include, taking periodical backup of data (to prevent theft or damage due to natural events such as floods, fire, etc.

Data Breach: Consulting firms handle an enormous volume of confidential client information. Such high-value information can be very damaging if it falls into the wrong hands. That makes professional service firms obvious targets for hackers, and data breaches, therefore, pose a particularly serious threat to consultancies.

In agriculture, some clients provide confidential data as input to carry out an analysis. Violation of these data can damage a consultant's reputation. In such a case if consulting business stores data in servers or cloud then it can be devastating. These actions can protect your business in case the servers are local and secured. Consultants should take reasonable steps to help prevent data breaches and other cyber-attacks. Best practices include:

- o Routinely taking back-up of project files, preferably on a separate hard disk or server.
- o Installing antivirus software on all systems.
- o Using complex passwords that are frequently changed.

Risk No. 3: Cash Flow

Cash flow is the inflow and outflow of money from a business. This enables it to settle debts, reinvest in its business, pay expenses, and provide a buffer against future financial challenges. Negative cash flow indicates that a company's liquid assets are decreasing. Cash flow also affects the company's ability to grow. Positive cash flow gives more capital to spend on expenditures like a new machine or new learnings or to undertake unpaid research work or on product development work. The more cash you bring in, the more freedom you get to reinvest.

Delayed Payment: It happens quite often that a consultant has performed his duties and submitted the invoice. It turns out that some clients pay late, if at all. You can reduce the chances of this happening by structuring your payments. For example, one could be activity-based payments, rather than waiting for 100 percent payment at the end of work. Second could be taking mobilization advance before the start of a project and then balance on deliverable-based payments. Carry out a proper agreement on payment terms.

Irregular Income Flow: There is a saying that "when it rains, it pours". When business is booming, you may have so many projects on your plate. You may turn some work away. But when work is scarce, the lack of work tends to expand. This can be due to any misfortune occurrence or due to market or can be due to natural hazards. Working as a consultant means accepting that your workload may fluctuate. A consultant can expect to face some level of risk. Acknowledging this risk ahead of time will help you handle it when it arrives.

Profitability: Clients are demanding greater value and flexibility at lower prices. This can hit the margins of consulting firms, forcing consultants to recalibrate their business models accordingly. This margin squeeze comes at a time when overhead costs, particularly travel, and contractor wages. The margin adjustment also arises, due to talent crunch. Some consulting firms look for low skill executives and charge client on high skill consultants, which in turn, results in a struggle with efficiency or lack control of their internal operations, feeling the pressure.

Risk No. 4: Health

Consultants or Small consulting firms face different challenges to their corporate counterparts. Income and financial uncertainty mean endlessly chasing work under changing economic conditions and owners feel responsible for the livelihoods of their staff. Consultants juggle multiple responsibilities, like sales, marketing purchases, and accounts.

In a consulting business, health plays an important role. One must be cautious about health issues with contractors and employees and specifically yourself. If the consultant is doing solo consulting, the consultant is the brand. He earns when he works and if due to illness, he stops working then the income stops.

The health of a consultant can connect to other risks. For example, due to il health of the consultant or his worker, the work gets delayed. This can lead to client unhappiness and further can delay the payments. Delayed payment can lead to poor cash flow that can slow down the growth of the company.

To be prepared for health risks, consider self-care as a solution. It is an investment. *"Self-care Leads to Long-term Business Success"*. The other solutions include the following.

- o Smart working: A plan of action keeps you focused, providing structure and a sense of achievement. Set up your day before you start by deciding what your priorities will be, what you want to achieve that day, and what can wait. Follow the important and urgent quadrant rule.

- o Avoid Distractions: Distractions can lead to a drop in productivity, so do not be afraid to turn off your phone and messages while you concentrate. It may feel odd but if you are consistent with checking emails at specific times and respond quickly, clients will be trained not to expect a response outside these hours.

- o Delegate and Outsource: When your business gets to a certain scale, find the resources to delegate or outsource things you're not great at. Not only will it create more time for you to grow the business and use your expertise better, but you also will not be stuck doing something you do not enjoy. Time spent training someone or purchasing a new system is an investment that will repay itself multiple times over; you gain efficiency and free up resources.

- o Stay Observant: Keep an eye to take notice of how your employees are feeling, whether stressed or enjoying. The quicker you identify stress, the quicker you can change things.

- o And most importantly, learn to say "no" if you do not believe you will achieve the right outcome for the client and yourself.

Risk No. 5: Market

A consultant can never guarantee stable income and predictable markets. Consultants must be prepared for uncertainty. Market ups and downs, shifting customer behaviors, and fluctuating volume of clients all contribute to unpredictable income. An unpredicted market can lead to a delay in client payments, and inconsistent business. Some steps can be taken to reduce the risk of market uncertainty such as:

- o Establish an emergency fund.

- o Set aside a portion of income as savings.

- o Specify payment terms and due dates in every client contract.

- o Stop depending on single clients: Too many small business owners fall into the trap of devoting all their time to their current clients.

Risk No. 6: New Competition

New players keep entering the consulting business sector. With new players, alternative and digital savvy solutions are being deployed. The new technologies enable them to do more with less concept. When you got into the market, you created the risk for other established consulting firms. Similarly, you are established as a consultant the new players create the challenge.

To stay in the market and to keep your clients intact, "defining competitive advantage" should be the priority of consultants. The increase in independent consultants is also proving to be a major competitive force. They put pressure on prices because they operate without the same overheads as the larger firms and can charge well below what the established consultancies can.

Another part of the consulting game is the rise of automation that allows customers to handle more of their complex problems in-house. This challenges the professional services sector, as it reduces the need to outsource. Clients can gain a much greater level of insight into how their profession works, either for free or at much lower prices, and can increasingly do so in real-time. With the rise of artificial intelligence, automation of consultancy work could become even more of a reality. Tasks performed by teams of smart junior analysts can today be carried out by a machine in the space of minutes.

Risk No. 7: Project Complexity

Scope creep is possibly the trickiest one of the risks in consulting business. Scope creep refers to changes, continuous or uncontrolled growth in a project's scope, at any point after the project begins. This can occur when the scope of a project is not properly defined, documented, or controlled. It is generally considered harmful.

The scope creep can happen due to the following reasons

When you are starting, you might get tempted to take additional scope of work only to avoid uncomfortable conversations with the client about money. This may seem like a good way to build your reputation with the customer, but it can backfire you with cost, time and resources overrun.

The other reason for cost creeping could be when no proper communication and documentation (agreement) done between customers and consultants.

One of the reasons could be, poor homework. If the consultant does not do proper homework or research before submitting the proposal, then scope creeping can happen.

One of the examples, I can tell from Dev's experience of working with a client. The client asked for Maize mapping in Indonesia for both the season (Dry and Wet). During the discussion, it was agreed that one set of images will be taken for the wet season and another for the dry season to map and estimated the maize growing areas. After the project was initiated and one set of images were taken for analysis, it was found with detailed research that the wet season planting period is about six months. Different provinces grow maize in different periods. Hence for the wet season itself, three sets of images were taken to do the analysis. This got added in the scope and additional time and money were spent on the work.

Another important reason to create project complexity is when a salesperson does the finalization of scope of work and at times overcommits (Committing beyond capability). This is quite common in the geospatial agriculture sector. To meet the sales target, the salesperson accepts the requirements that are beyond the team's capability and later ends up either underdelivering or spending more on the project than expected.

To prevent consultant scope creep, take the following steps:

- o Detail scope of work, all project deliverables, and expectations in the client proposal first and later bring the same in the contract.
- o Communicate project progress updates
- o Discuss if any issues arise (For example, in Dev's case, if he would have done proper agreement, the additional work could have benefited the customer as well as Dev).

- o Clearly define clauses for change of scope scenario, payment terms, damage due to natural hazards, etc., in terms and conditions.

- o Involve technical team (consultant) in sales discussion and project scope of work finalization.

It can be hard to say no to a client, but the costs of extending projects and giving away work can quickly add up. If you do not keep an eye out for scope creep, it could put your financial goals at risk.

Risk No. 8: Partner consultants and team Issues

Consulting projects rely on experts' thought processes to fuel their innovative ideas into the project. Consulting projects also rely on the team to execute large size geospatial agriculture projects such as field survey for crops and land use, image processing, digitization work, analysis, and documentation. Therefore, people are crucial to the industry. However, this system is exceptionally vulnerable to human error and issues.

Handling these vulnerabilities can be a laborious task. Employees and partners come with challenges also such as compensation issues health issues, availability issues (if not employed), infrastructure issues, etc. One must take care of the team so that team can take care of the business.

The qualities and skills of being a team player, communication, listening skills can play an important role in handling team issues and solving them efficiently.

Risk No. 9: Reputational Damage

As a consultant your character, your status, and your reputation are everything. The consulting business works two ways: Word-of-mouth referrals tend to generate business, while dissatisfied clients spreading the word can hinder your ability to get new clients or can have a chance to lose existing ones. The consultant must make sure you fulfill your role as agreed upon in the contract. If there is an issue or dispute, communicate it upfront and solve it in coordination with the customer. In case the customer role is not required in the issue then keep them informed and solve the issue. Property damage can be solved with money but to bring back the status takes a long time.

> *"It takes 20 years to build a reputation and few minutes of cyber-incident to ruin it."*
>
> **– Stephane Nappo**

Chapter 10

Reason of Consulting Business Failure

"You learn more from failure than from success. Do not let it stop you. Failure builds character"

No one, whether in business, consulting, job, or studies would like to fail. Everyone wants to succeed. We follow successful people. There will be hundreds or thousands of books available, teaching success formula. But if we go deep into a successful business or successful people, we can find somewhere they would have failed. These failure incidences need to be taken as lessons to move forward. One needs to work on the causes of failure so that, he can move ahead in step to success. But he should not repeat or ignore the causes. If done so, then it is definite for your business to fail.

Success and failure, however, are terms meant to define events, not people. You are either successful at doing something or achieving some milestone, or you failed at doing something or did not achieve some milestone. That does not imply that you are a complete success or a complete failure.

Consulting is more of an individual's skill-based work. Consulting is a good business. It is enjoyable, exciting, profitable, and it helps people. As a consultant, you must become indispensable to thrive in this fast-growing, highly competitive, and digital market. Consulting is a relationship business, and to succeed as a consultant, you must have an effective and far-reaching network of professional relationships. An experienced consultant is impeccable by developing areas of expertise and works on soft skills to build relationships and provide optimal service to clients. A less experienced consultant might slip and overstate capabilities due to need, greed, or naivety. Most of the consultants or consulting firms work out well. But many of these small consulting companies fail to grow.

> *"Eighty-five percent of the reasons for failure are deficiencies in the systems and process rather than the employee. The role of management is to change the process rather than badgering individuals to do better."*
>
> **– W. Edwards Deming**

There are many reasons by which consultants do not get the results and fail. In this section, we will discuss the nine most common reasons for consulting business failure. This chapter is all about why a consultant or a consulting firm fails.

Reason No.1: Incompetency

This is one of the most common reasons you will observe in the failure of geospatial agriculture projects or any other business. Companies working models have changed to *"More with Less"* formulae. Companies hire resources from college and are directly put into live projects. As college pass out freshers are paid much less than any experienced person, hence can look for better project profitability. This leads to poor quality project output or delay in delivery or can even ruin the project.

If we look at the individuals getting into freelancing or solo consulting. Some individuals with their college knowledge and childhood dream of "not to work for any boss" get into the consulting business without having any experience fail to understand the client's need completely. Similarly, some individuals have experience working in image processing and GIS projects but do not have agriculture subject knowledge that fails to understand the need completely.

Every year we find new companies get into the Geospatial agriculture consulting business and after few years they are either closed or get diversified to another sector. The reason is their Incomplete Expertise: If a consultant or consulting team does not thoroughly understand what it takes to examine and execute a successful project, it can result in poor delivery to a client problem.

To avoid consulting failure, the consultant must gain adequate knowledge and experience. Consultants must keep learning the subject and new technologies. Keep assessing your capabilities. Even clients should assess the capabilities of the company who they hire who agrees to provide the solution.

While it can be difficult, both the client and consultant need to identify the capabilities of anyone at the company who may be potentially involved with implementation. Without understanding the essential processes and tasks involved with new consulting engagements and the capabilities of those responsible, unexpected barriers can impede success early on. An experienced consultant will know to confirm in the agreement who will do what and what is expected.

Reason No. 2: Self Orientation

Self-orientation is all about where your attention is focused. It is about focusing on your interests, rather than the client's needs. This is related to incompetency. If you have less knowledge or less experience, you focus more on what you know or what you have, rather than what the other person needs. When you operate from high self-orientation, you do not hear others. You do not hear their questions, desires, fears, or emotions in general. If your attention is focused on your product or solution, others become aware of it and infer that you do not care about their problems. This makes them decide that you are untrustworthy.

Conversely, if your level of self-orientation is low, you can pay attention to someone else. If you pay attention to someone, they experience that as caring. If someone thinks you care about them, they are likely to trust you.

The most basic principle of successful consulting is to sell what your client wants to buy. If you avoid the most common mistakes and instead focus on results that matter to your clients, you can develop a thriving business and make a greater impact. This will make clients know you and trust your work

Reason No. 3: Failing to build relation

Most the consulting business or consultant's fail because they project themselves as more transactional. For example, submitting a financial proposal immediately after your first meeting with the client and then keep on following up for closure. In this case, the actual problem of the client is not understood. Another example is presenting only your products and detailing product specifications and their benefits. Rather than asking if the customer is interested in it or not. It is more of pushing your product to the customer. The relation is over once the product is sold to a customer.

To avoid the failure of consulting business, you must cultivate transformative relationships. It means that you are not being observed as a commodity where the client leaves the money, and you do the work.

Transactional relationships are more economic and functional. They are based on the exchange of money, goods, or services. When that service has been fulfilled, the relationship ends. A transformational relationship is a relationship that focuses more on problem-solving and care for the other.

"I think for any relationship to be successful, there needs to be loving communication, appreciation, and understanding."

– **Miranda Kerr**

Dan Lok always tells his students – people buy because of what you sell, but they stay with you because of who you are. This means that you need to nurture and strengthen your relationships with clients. This is what distinguishes you from your competition. It is all about how you made them *feel*. Often it has way less to do with the quality of your work and much more with the quality of the relationship you built.

It is difficult to generate consistent income with transactional relations. Whereas a long-term relationship can be built with transformational relation. The reason to fail in building a good relationship with a client could be any of the following:

- o The pressure of sales target by CEO on the salesperson to close the deal
- o Not having enough projects in hand. This makes a consultant think about cash flow
- o Lack of consulting mindset
- o Lack of knowledge and qualities of consultant

Your relationship with the client and how you make them feel is as important as what you sell.

Reason No. 4: Pricing

If you, *"Price your product too high and you'll push away potential customers, too low and you won't be able to turn a profit."*

Pricing decisions can have incredibly significant consequences for consulting projects. A wrong price decision can damage the competency trust of a client with a consultant. It is extremely significant to fix prices at the right level after a detailed understanding of client problems, sufficient research, and evaluation of factors like cost of execution (resources), competitors, long-term relationships with the same client, more business generation through this client, etc.

Low prices may attract customers in the initial stages, but it would be difficult for the consultant to raise prices on a future date. Similarly, a high price will ensure more profit margins but will have lesser sales. Hence, to maintain a balance between profitability and volume of sales, it is important to fix the right price.

Reason No. 5: Lack of internal support

This is one of the critical reasons for the failure of a consultant in the geospatial agriculture business. As a consultant, you need to be a team player. Many projects cannot be done alone it needs a team. In geospatial agriculture projects, we need agriculture experts, GIS experts, image processing experts, field surveyors, application developers, support of finance, and administrations, etc. Regardless of the knowledge, expertise, enthusiasm, and passion, a consultant can bring to a project, when it becomes noticeable that those involved are not in full support with the execution of tasks, the project failure is obvious. And it quickly becomes "the consultant's fault."

It makes sense that it is the responsibility of the company to ensure ample research is done before hiring a consultant. Likewise, the consultant should also do a detailed capability assessment of the team members before getting involved in any assignment.

Team Conflict: Despite the best intentions of the company, as well as the best efforts put in by the team members, the consultants or consulting teams still fail. This could be due to various reasons.

- o Location: The team members may be placed at different locations making it difficult for them to meet frequently. Tim zone could be a reason for the communication gap. Communication is vital for any team to work well. Physical distances can always be overcome with the use of technology. Hence a solution needs to be found to resolve this issue.

- o Misaligned resources: The consultant is not given adequate resources to do the job. You cannot expect an employee to work with his hands tied, can you? Also, when the team is not aligned to the project goal. Everybody will do their own thing with no attention to team goals. Working in silos leads to duplication of work.

- o Position and roles: At times position and role of an individual can clash with the responsibilities assigned. If personal styles are different and causing conflict among team members, a consultant should use a behavioral assessment tool to help people better understand each other and learn to work together.

Reason No. 6: Project Execution

This is a quite common formula. If you do not read for examination, you fail. If you do not learn and practice driving a car, you may meet with an accident. If you do not prepare for your training, your students may not learn. Be it your school, or business; if you do not do your job well, you will fail. Likewise, in the geospatial agriculture consulting business if you do not execute the projects effectively you will fail to get more business or clients.

This failure in execution can happen due to issues with both clients and consultants. Major challenges include defining problems, understanding the scope of work, lack of well-qualified resources, and lack of communication.

Consultants need to develop processes for new areas of expertise, join hands with other experts to build the practice area expertise, and be upfront with potential clients to ensure adaptability and to manage expectations. The other lesson is to simply not over-state capabilities and sells things you do not know how to do. Do not overcommit and underperform.

Another reason for failure due to poor execution is the emphasis on business strategy. More emphasis is given on sales, business development, and marketing strategy. Whereas less focus will be on execution/operational strategy. This can be due to over-confidence.

Reason No. 7: Not listening

In consulting business, poor listening or no listening can lead to misunderstanding, poor service delivery, and an unhappy client. Poor listening leads to errors, ineffective decisions, and/or costly mistakes. You cannot have a "know it all" attitude and expect to discover and understand critical pain points that will allow you to provide relevant analysis. By not listening, or by ignoring what your client says, you will miss key factors inhibiting your ability to make the best recommendations.

As a consultant if you listen well, you can understand well, you can define the problem well, you can document well, and finally, you can serve well. The different causes of poor listening are distractive minds, jumping to a conclusion, interruptions, and not paying close attention to the speaker. Listening is one of the important business communication skills. When a client feels they are being listened to, they feel respected and cared. This can lead to sharing of more and valuable information by a client. Good listening is crucial to maintain a productive relationship and with the client sometimes it is the only good way to establish communication.

Statistics indicate that the normal untrained listener is likely to understand and retain only about 50 percent of the conversation. This relatively poor percentage drops to an even less impressive 25 percent retention rate 48 hours later. This means that recall of conversations will usually be inaccurate and incomplete unless you were attentively listening for a purpose.

Not talking or responding to the client in the conversation does not mean to be silent completely. Silence digs your career grave. Synthesize what is being said. This is an invaluable skill and doesn't require new insight. Simply take a few important points while actively listening and sum them up, on the pretext of trying to understand the conversation.

Reason No. 8: Reluctant to do low paid activities

"It's your attitude at the beginning, that decides your failure or success"

Many experts and consultants are being misguided for not doing low paid projects. They are told *"raise the bar"*. *"low paid job will lower their status in the industry"*, *"do only high-ticket consulting"* etc. Consulting is all about your knowledge and expertise. To gain expertise a consultant must-do projects to build case studies. Here we do not say that consultants do the job at loss, but with fewer profit projects can be done. Early on, every new coach or consultant must separate themselves from the crowd. The best way is to gain as much project working experience as possible. These are a form of credibility to a consultant. These are brand-building activities for a consultant. Yet many consultants, who were used to the high-level corporate salaries that they left behind, are often reluctant to do the free or low-fee work that is necessary for the early days to build credibility and brand.

At times free or low fee jobs can build the client relationship and open the doors to other bigger projects. Likewise, showing unwillingness towards such projects can spoil the relationship with clients. If a consultant fails initially due to this, it will be difficult for him to get back as other competitors would have grown bigger by then.

On the other side, a consultant must be smart enough to judge clients. He should not continue to work at a low price once he has established his credibility in the industry. There will be price-sensitive clients who only value you for your low price. You will get low-value projects from them, and they will only refer you to other low-budget clients.

Reason No. 9: Taking primary clients for granted

Client retention in the consulting business is extremely important, but too much dependency on one or few clients can be dangerous. The current economic climate has seen some firms lose clients unexpectedly. While some of the departures may be a blessing in disguise, some may be a shock.

Consultants fail if they are too dependent on a few clients - Pareto's 80-20 rule applies to consulting firms as well, especially for small firms. A few clients will bring in the majority of revenue and losing such clients is often enough to sink the firm. Also, building effective client relationships is difficult in consulting. A study by Forbes indicated that only half of consulting clients used the same firm again after a project. This is even though 92% of clients were happy with the firms they hired. This just indicates that building client relationships is a complex process and not just limited to executing projects.

Taking the customer for granted is one of all strategic mistakes the consultant makes. A consultant is blinded by growth and starts to believe that whatever products or services in need, their customers will always be there to buy them. This does not apply in today's world, as competition catches up quickly with fast-growing businesses. This means that customers will search elsewhere for value when businesses fail to meet their expectations, or they become greedy.

A consultant must take consistent action to protect his territory. He must take nothing for granted. Every customer and every relationship are at risk. A consultant must take systematic action to strengthen client relationships and equally strengthen the value of his solution or service.

Reason No. 10: Failing to do networking, marketing, and brand building for future business

Consulting is all about relations and connections. Professional networking is an important element to the success of consulting business. It can help you meet people, gain information, make useful contacts, find opportunities, get referrals, and generate new leads.

Michael Zipurskey of consulting success says, Networking in the business consulting industry is very crucial but an often-overlooked part of many people's marketing plan. There is an old saying that goes *"it is not what you know, it is who you know."* That saying could not be truer so you need to get out there and start networking and making connections!

Michael further says that networking is about building relationships, obtaining and giving referrals, and building your reputation, and because of that, the potential impact on your business is directly proportionate to the number of professional network contacts you have. Consider it from a purely mathematical standpoint. Your professional network consists of ten people. Each of those ten people has ten other contacts of their own. That means you have direct access to ten potential clients and indirect access to an additional one hundred!

We all know that you need to build your brand. Networking for a consultant is the equivalent of a company using marketing to build its brand. It is the key to success. Done correctly, networking will allow you to promote yourself and build your brand and reputation. Networking should be a priority for all of us. You will become a known commodity among key players in a variety of consulting firms. Even if you feel that you do not require a network now, you must understand that establishing a network is essential in the current competitive business world. When done tactfully and effectively, networking can take your brand to the next level, which in turn can boost your career.

Reason No. 11: Lack of Integrity.

According to motivational speaker and author Brian Tracy:

"Whenever I hold a strategic planning session, the first value that all the executives agree on is integrity. Leaders know that honesty and integrity are the foundations of leadership. Leaders stand up for what they believe in."

Credibility, trust, and respect are important in all healthy relationships. By ignoring the importance and impact of integrity, you risk failure. You cannot be dishonest, manipulative, abusive, or negligent and still expect to be rewarded. These days, most business owners understand the importance of integrity in business. After all, words like "authenticity," "trustworthiness" and "transparency" are prominent on company websites and throughout marketing materials.

A consultant's integrity is reflected by the way he does the business. Some of the practices that lack integrity include:

- o Not treating every customer with the same respect
- o Mistreating partner experts, staff, or contractors

- o Misleading clients or misrepresenting your services and abilities
- o Overselling and under-delivering

Integrity can get you a stronger reputation, client satisfaction, quality of your results to the customer, better culture, and stronger sales. Lack of this can lead to failure.

> *"Consultants are not Superheroes that they do not do mistakes. They do and fail at times. But a good, trusted, and impeccable consultant is one who learns from his failures, improves on the mistakes, and moves on"*

Move to Problem Solving Action – Start Consulting

My thanks to all readers. To be a leading light as a consultant you need to bring your knowledge and expertise to the business table. If you want to stand out and be indispensable in today's world then it includes your personality, your tribe, and most importantly your purpose to serve.

> *"Try not become a person of success, but rather try to become a person of value"*

To get into consulting, access your strength and skillset, shift your mindset to consulting with a purpose to serve and solve problems, be a problem solver and create value for the customer, follow a consultative selling approach, build a relation, and avoid being transactional in consulting, invest in learning and developing tools for your business and finally stay organized and deliver results

> *"Create value ……Create more value……become indispensable"*

As a trusted consultant, you should grow others. You should become replaceable. So that you grow and become indispensable. Be focused, be genuine, be consistent and live your brand as leading light (the geospatial agriculture consultant). You do not need a perfect team or boss to become an impeccable consultant. You become the leading light and you will make the perfect team and get a perfect boss.

"Don't be a spectator, be a leading light in the stage called-world."

References

The idea of sharing my experience through this book was like a seed. It has to grow to a full plant and give fruits to others. To grow the seed, it needs manure that can nourish it with the nutrition of knowledge. This knowledge could not have been fulfilled without reading books and articles of some great authors. I am thankful to them and I hope to keep learning from them. Some of the books and articles that I read during my writing process of this book are mentioned below.

Books

- o "Linchpin", by Seth Godin
- o "The leader who has no Title", by Robin Sharma
- o "The 5 AM Club" by Robin Sharma
- o "Leader who has no title" by Robin Sharma
- o "Think and Grow Rich", by Nepolean Hill
- o "The magic of Thinking Big", David Joseph
- o "Start with Why", by Simon Sinek
- o "80% mindset and 20% skillset", by Dev Gadvi
- o "Lead or bleed", by Rajiv Talreja
- o "Blink" by Malcom Gladwil

- o "Starting and running a successful consultancy", by Susan Nash
- o "The trusted advisor", by David H. Maister, Charles H. Green, Robert M. Galford
- o "Blue ocean shift" by W. Chan Kim and Renee Mauborgne

Youtube videos

- o Consulting Success, by Michael Zipurskey
- o Motivational talks by Sandeep Maheshwari
- o Bada Business, by Vivek Bindra
- o Project Manager.com

Mentoring

- o Jyotsna Ramachandran of Author Success Academy

Ebooks and articles

- o Building a Successful Consulting Practice: Opportunities and Challenges; By Patti P. Phillips, Ph.D., and Jack J. Phillips, Ph.D. (This article originally appeared in Building a Successful Consulting Practice, ASTD, 2004)
- o Consulting In The New Economy: How to Start, Run and Grow A Successful Consulting Business in 2020. Michael Zipursky. consultingsuccess.com
- o Getting started in consulting. Third Edition Book by Alan Weiss. Published by John Wiley & Sons, Inc., Hoboken, New Jersey. Published simultaneously in Canada.
- o Abundant Entrepreneur, Sabrina

o Consulting 101: 101 Tips for Success in Consulting, by Lew Sauder

o Building a Successful Consulting Practice: Opportunities and Challenges by By Patti P. Phillips, Ph.D., and Jack J. Phillips, PhD

"NO CANDLE LOSES ITS LIGHT WHILE LIGHTING ANOTHER CANDLE.

NEVER STOP SHARING, CARING AND HELPING OTHERS, BECAUSE IT MAKES OUR LIFE MORE MEANINGFUL"

SENSING AGRICULTURE FROM SPACE

Geospatial technology concepts and solutions for key players in agri value chain

DINESH KAR

www.ingramcontent.com/pod-product-compliance
Lightning Source LLC
Chambersburg PA
CBHW030942180526
45163CB00002B/670